C000241712

"Sue Atkinson spells out with costly [...]
No illusions or shortcuts, but a powe[...]
promises and imperatives actually fles[...]
shown how what seems impossible be[...]
of 'magical' swiftness and ease, so that [...]love of
Christ never moves out of focus. A book of real value and depth."

Most Revd Dr Rowan Williams, *former Archbishop of Canterbury*

"*Struggling to Forgive* is a book which, as its title so aptly points out, is honest
that forgiveness can be a struggle, and at times a very hard struggle. Well-
informed by pastoral realism and theological integrity, Sue Atkinson leads
us through many difficult questions to do with forgiveness with plenty of
real-life examples. I warmly commend this perceptive book as thought-
provoking, easy to read and eminently practical."

Dr Anthony Bash, *Hatfield College, Durham University*

"Christians are often confused – not least by their pastors – about what it
means to forgive and when it's appropriate. Mercifully free of glib cliché,
Sue Atkinson's book offers us a refreshingly honest, psychologically realistic,
biblically responsible, and pastorally sensitive account of the varieties and
complexities of forgiveness. Admirably clear in its writing and digestible
in its organisation, *Struggling to Forgive* marries the wisdom of messy
experience with thoughtful Christian reflection to produce plausible
practical advice, both for those who struggle and for those who seek to help
them. Many will find it a godsend."

Nigel Biggar, *Regius Professor of Moral and Pastoral Theology, Oxford
University*

"In this personal and passionate book, informed by difficult experience
and extensive reading, Sue Atkinson tells the story not so much of her
personal struggle to forgive, as of a larger struggle which involves coming to
understand why and how so much preaching and teaching about forgiveness
is unhelpful.

With remarkable restraint she pares back the crude mechanistic teaching
that re-abuses victims by inflicting on them a need for a mechanical and
fear-filled forgiveness, and then opens the door to true forgivingness which
is usually slow and always accompanied by compassion, healing, uncertainty

and all the other hallmarks of mature and realistic Christian living.

Accessible and honest, this is a book based on hard-won self-awareness and genuine compassion for others. It can therefore be placed with gentle confidence in the hands of victims of abuse - and perhaps more forcibly presented to those who have yet to understand that pastoral ministry is properly focussed on a creative 'could', not a threat-laden 'must.'"

> **Canon Dr Stephen Cherry,** *author of* Healing Agony: Reimagining Forgiveness

"A very good and illuminating read. A wonderful achievement. Sue Atkinson writes about the complexity of forgiveness with striking honesty and profound simplicity. Those struggling to forgive will be helped to understand themselves. Anyone inclined to instruct others to forgive will be chastened. People able to forgive will be given fresh insight into what they have done. Sue addresses our minds and spirits with great sensitivity. She has written a forgiving book."

> **Rt Revd Graham James,** *Lord Bishop of Norwich*

"Forgiveness is a huge word to confront as a survivor of child abuse or childhood trauma. Sue Atkinson has brilliantly examined the problems associated with this word for survivors within the context of Christianity.

My hope is that this book is not only read by survivors of child abuse but also by caring Christians who are interested in genuinely helping people to heal from the hurts of their childhood. Thank you, Sue, for once again bringing light and Christian insight to help survivors of abuse on their healing journey."

> **Liz Mullinar,** *founder of The Heal for Life Foundation, Australia*

STRUGGLING TO FORGIVE

Moving on from trauma

Sue Atkinson

MONARCH
BOOKS

Oxford, UK & Grand Rapids, Michigan, USA

Published by Monarch Books
an imprint of
Lion Hudson plc
Wilkinson House, Jordan Hill Road,
Oxford OX2 8DR, England
Email: monarch@lionhudson.com
www.lionhudson.com/monarch

ISBN 978 0 85721 561 1
e-ISBN 978 0 85721 562 8

First edition 2014

Acknowledgments
Scripture quotations (unless otherwise stated) are from The New Revised
Standard Version of the Bible copyright © 1989 by the Division of Christian
Education of the National Council of Churches in the USA. Used by
permission. All Rights Reserved.
Scripture taken from *The Message*. Copyright © by Eugene H. Peterson, 1993,
1994, 1995, 1996. Used by permission of NavPress Publishing Group.

A catalogue record for this book is available from the British Library.

Printed and bound in the UK, June 2014, LH26

The many stories in this book are all based on real incidents. However, please
note that key details such as names and places have been changed to protect
confidentiality.

Contents

Section C

Section D

FOR A, WITH MY LOVE.

By the same author

Breaking the Chains of Abuse

Building Self-Esteem

Climbing out of Depression

First Steps out of Depression

In Times of Need

Pathways Through Depression

Jonah's Whale of a Time Book

Mrs Noah's Rainy Day Book

Acknowledgments

Over the eleven years I have been writing this book a great many people have helped me. Some of them were in groups I convened, and knew they were helping me, but others were people in workshops I was running, or attending, or just talking about their lives and the struggles they were having following some devastating experiences.

Thank you so much for sharing part of your life. Being able to weave together so many different experiences helped me enormously to get a wide view of the effects of traumatic incidents, and to think through what forgiveness means as we learn how we recover from them and walk free of our burdens.

In some ways this book is a sequel to my book *Breaking the Chains of Abuse*. It was as I researched that book that the problematic nature of forgiveness became clear, and I knew I had to explore further.

I've greatly valued comments from the various clergy groups I've had the privilege of leading while sharing thoughts on how to respond well to survivors of abuse, and what forgiving might mean in that context. My special thanks to my colleague Carolyn Buckeridge, whose wisdom and friendship over many years has supported me as I worked through demanding issues in difficult settings. Thanks also to Janet Craske of the Methodist Church, who I heard talk about forgiving in the context of domestic abuse in a way which I found incredibly helpful.

I couldn't possibly have completed this book without the support and help of David, my husband. We've spent years hammering out ideas, and his theological and pastoral insights have been crucial. And helping me in the final stages actually to finish the script was amazing. You're a great "completer/finisher"! Thank you.

Thank you also to both Andrew Hodder-Williams and Tony Collins of Lion Hudson/Monarch. First for liking the book enough to publish it! And second, for your insightful editorial comments which enabled me to stand back from the text and think again about the central issues.

My thanks to Joy Dunn for the evocative illustrations.

Thank you also to three special women: Anne Townsend and Kate Litchfield, who have helped me enormously as I've struggled to understand what forgiving means for me and for others. And Penny Bird, who listened, suggested, shared her thoughts and kept encouraging me.

Finally, for keeping me sane over the last few years of the book, thanks to my lovely friend Gwyneth Chatten, the best and wisest triathlon training partner ever. Finishing this book was just like us cycling up Fire Mountain! We got there in the end. And thank you Tanja Slater for being such an inspirational coach and for helping me do things I never thought I could. That's good training for learning to forgive and how to live a good life!

Sue Atkinson, London, February 2014

Foreword by Elaine Storkey

There is so often a yawning gap between the wisdom and compassion of the Christian Gospel and the way Christians think and speak. This is so evident in the issue of forgiveness. There is no doubt that forgiveness is at the very heart of Christianity. It is what God offers us through Christ; an expression of God's mercy and love that we can be restored into a healed relationship. And when we are able to forgive one another we see something of God's grace in action among us, and know that sin does not have the last word. But the act of forgiving requires depth and that depth is often missing in the glib way we respond to those who have been damaged by others. Far too often we rush to insist that they should forgive, without reflecting on what this actually means in their lives, how it connects with emotional upheaval, and their battle for self-understanding. And far from releasing these people into the liberating power of the Gospel, our easy words can drag them further into bondage.

For what is it for human beings to forgive? What does it require from us, and how do we understand the processes of forgiveness in the context of a broken or fragile life? There are times when we are incapable of forgiving, not because we do not want to forgive, but because we do not have the emotional or mental capacity to reach out beyond pain and confusion. Forgiveness needs to be part of healing, not a denial of the reality or severity of suffering. Serious wrong inflicted on a person's life can have terrible and far-reaching consequences.

These issues and so many more are the subject matter of this book. The author looks carefully at many areas of brokenness and defeat and the long-term effects of trauma in a person's experience. She examines the struggle for self-worth, and the legacy of violation which makes the process of forgiving complicated and confusing. She exposes the many strands of "weird Christian thinking" which direct practices within many churches and leaves the vulnerable stranded and isolated. She probes the different effects of passivity and anger and urges us to recognize how these affect not just our ability to forgive, but the reshaping of what forgiveness means.

Her analysis of the relationship between forgiveness and justice is a neglected enquiry among Christians. The need for justice is often swept aside in the belief that forgiveness is a more spiritual requirement. Yet it becomes clear that if the integrity of the Gospel is to be made evident, the two cannot be polarized. They sit together as significant aspects of the journey towards greater wholeness.

The honesty of this book is self-evident. It recognizes, from the perspective of a believer, the costly nature of being a disciple of Christ. But it is also a plea for a more authentic and compassionate biblical understanding. Theology is interwoven with psychology as an integrated whole; the text is peppered with narrative and many stories are alarmingly close to home. Yet the crucial points are drawn out with compassion and gentleness. The book models the message it offers. Human beings are precious; many of us need healing, and to be helped to forgive. But we must never block people's way to God's love by distorting what true forgiveness means, and the journey we must take to reach it.

Preface

Much of my motivation for writing this book came from talking with groups of mainly Christian people who had been through traumatic and abusive experiences. Some had been told by their pastors that they must forgive or God wouldn't forgive them – sometimes with clear warning that struggling to forgive wasn't good enough – even being told "you are going to hell".

Understandably, for some, this felt like being abused all over again, and during discussions about forgiving, I encountered many tearful and muddled people. And as I listened, rage began to grow inside me. I realized I was surrounded by very confused people who had been treated appallingly.

How could pastors and "Christian counsellors" behave like this? I felt it was totally inappropriate to tell someone they are going to hell – particularly when the person is struggling with the effects of trauma and mental health issues.

Exploring forgiving

I spent many years reading about forgiving and talking to groups, and it was interesting that some Christians seemed to feel that forgiving was something that was easy and straightforward – a totally different view from that of people who had experienced some devastatingly difficult event.

For example, one day I was sitting with a group of Christian friends drinking tea, and someone asked me what I was working on at the moment. I said I was writing about forgiveness and

Mavis said: "If only everyone would just forgive, the world would be a much better place." Everyone nodded in agreement (including me, because it sounds exactly right and everyone was looking at me so I thought I should!). But later, when I'd thought about it, I asked one of the friends whether it would have been right in the 1930s just to let Hitler invade Poland? Should the politicians have just forgiven him? "I see what you mean," my friend said. "I never thought of that."

Since that time I've engaged a great many individuals and groups in discussions about forgiving, including issues such as how forgiveness might relate to justice, and I found that the simplistic "Why doesn't everyone just forgive?" belief is widespread, particularly amongst Christians.

Yes, it sounds right. But it can't possibly be right! It's very much more complicated than that, and implying that forgiving is easy, if only we would try harder, usually makes things very much worse.

Trauma and forgiveness

This book is an exploration of what forgiveness means, especially following some kind of trauma – for example, a hit and run accident, burglary, domestic violence, murder or abuse.

I've illustrated these examples in a series of stories. The stories are all about things that have actually happened, but I've often merged several stories together and disguised the circumstances, settings and people to protect identities. The core of the book is reflections on what these stories imply about forgiveness and justice.

I will explore some of the Christian teaching that can cause so much anxiety for those who have been through a traumatic incident, and offer some suggestions for practical responses and pastoral care.

As I talked to people about their experiences, some spoke of their burdens and how they felt weighed down by life. So I've used this image throughout the book and have suggested some strategies for ways we might seek to put down our heavy backpack to ease our journey through life.

SECTION A

In this first section I lay out some of my initial thinking about the book and show the complexities of what forgiving involves.

Contrary to popular Christian belief, forgiving isn't the answer to every difficult situation. It isn't a quick fix. It isn't easy or straightforward for people who have experienced devastating events.

CHAPTER 1

How Do We Start to Think About What Forgiving Means?

I wonder what we actually do when we forgive?

(Victoria)

I sat down to make a start on this book on 7 July 2005. I'd done some reading. I had piles of notes beside me and wanted to get some initial writing to the editor so that she could see the direction my proposed book might take.

The phone rang. It was my husband, David. He'd heard the news of bombs in London on the car radio.

"Ring the kids now," he said. "Find out if they are all safe."

Immediately a day of phone calls, emails and terrible television news starts. My heart pounds and, close to tears, I ring David back to report that the family are all safe. But our daughter Rachel and her husband Nick are just a couple of blocks from the bus explosion in their offices above their church.

I sit with my notes for this book in front of me, staring at the television. All I can think of is if my daughter, seven months pregnant with her first child, had been blown up, how would I ever have been able to forgive the bombers?

How could anyone forgive those bombers?

My friend Victoria rings and we talk about the bombs and forgiveness. She says: "What do we actually do when we forgive?"

We discuss this for a bit and I realize this is an important question. If Rachel and her baby had been blown apart, what is it that I might have had to work through?

Anger?

Yes, I know that is what I would feel. How could I possibly feel otherwise? The Archbishop of Canterbury, Rowan Williams, comes on the television with his message from himself and the Muslims he is talking to that day. He talks of our prayers for those bereaved or injured. He also talks about our anger. Yes. We are right to be filled with rage that some people decided, for whatever reason, to blow up innocent bystanders of all faiths, of all ages.

Furious rage is an appropriate reaction.

Forgiveness seems to me to be out of the question.

I stare at my notes for this book. I thought I was close to being able at least to make a start on it. But the past few hours have shown me I'm a very long way from that.

Someone lost their baby

My "baby" is safe. Her unborn baby is safe. But as news filters through, the body count begins to rise.

There is a mother somewhere who is weeping. Her "baby" has been blown up.

Rachel rings . They have opened up the church for cups of tea, a place for people to be safe – and to let distressed people use the land phone lines because all the mobile phone connections are jammed. Everyone just wants to connect with their loved ones. "Are you safe? I love you." The last messages of the victims on planes on 11 September 2001 have stuck in our memories.

At a major crisis point, we all just want to say, "I love you."

Rachel and Nick are exhausted and want me to pray for them all. Their vicar and the curate have gone out into the streets to bring comfort, and point people towards the cups of tea at the church. I know those two men will face traumatic scenes. I ring a friend I've known for years to see if her children are safe.

Emails flood in. "Yes," I reply, "they are all safe."

Forgiveness after major trauma

Also this week there have been the sixtieth anniversary celebrations and memorial services for the end of World War Two in Asia. On television people who had been prisoners of war in Japan are talking about forgiving the torture and the brutality. One man says he could never forgive because what was done was unforgivable. Another says he forgave long ago and his face shows his sense of peace.

Those old soldiers will have something in common with the people who by the end of today will be grieving or looking for a lost loved one in a hospital.

All of them will face the challenge of how to get their lives back.

How will they go on?

Will they ever be happy again?

Will they be able to forgive?

Will they want to forgive?

Is it even appropriate for them to forgive?

I start to write in my journal to try to make sense of what I'm feeling.

Forgiving is difficult

It is extraordinary how much of the world we live in seems to hold contradictory beliefs. "Forgive and forget" is what is said so often. You hear them on the soap operas. "You've got to move on," the character says. "Tomorrow is another day."

The victim looks unsure.

Soap operas, just like life, seem to be printed all the way through, like seaside rock, with the words "anger" and "resentment".

I understand these contradictory beliefs. All day I've been saying to myself, "You kill my 'baby' and you die."

Those are words I found myself saying years ago when my daughter was thirteen years old and had to cycle through a dark and dangerous-looking underpass on her way to school. I feared for her safety and realized that if I was with her and someone attacked her, I would tear the attacker apart.

This had shocked me because I had thought at that time that I was a pacifist.

I realized that humans, in a confusing and ambiguous world, can hold these conflicting views. So finding myself today doing my "hurt my 'baby' and you die" thinking, focused me onto the huge problem that humans have when someone does something extremely hurtful.

If you accidentally bump into me and you say, "Sorry!" I turn and say, "That's fine, I'm OK." It is so trivial I will not be thinking about it beyond the next few moments.

If you deliberately bump into me, but still (eventually) say, "Sorry!" I would find that harder to forgive, but I would hardly lose sleep over it. (Unless it was part of a family or other feud with far-reaching effects.) I would probably be able to forgive you in time.

But if you torture me, or blow up my loved ones, or kidnap and imprison me, or rape me, or mentally abuse and manipulate me, that is totally different. Forgiveness in these circumstances is much more complex. And Victoria's question – What do we actually do when we forgive? – needs exploring.

Instant forgiving

I admire those who can do "instant forgiving" after some trauma. I was so impressed by the responses of Gee Walker a few years ago when she forgave the young men who killed her son Anthony in a racist attack. She cared about those killers and she knew something had happened to them that had turned them into murderers at such a young age. She coped well with a reporter holding a microphone to her face and asking, "Do you forgive?"

I know that if today my child had died and a reporter asked me if I forgave the bombers, I would probably have yelled at him through my tears and rage.

Resentment can be awful. We probably all know people who have become "bitter and twisted" about something in their life; being around them can be uncomfortable at best, and excruciating at worst.

So what does it mean "not to hold grudges"? What do we actually do when we try to forgive someone? And do we have to forgive, as some believe?

Every day

My thinking about forgiving has been strongly influenced by Gee Walker, as I mentioned above. Several months after her son was killed, she was asked if she was still able to forgive the murders. She talked about how forgiving was "every day... oh... every day".

Yes, this is how forgiving is for me and for people I've talked to about their struggles, and this "every day" theme runs throughout this book.

Key points

- "Why can't some people just forgive?" is a common question, implying that forgiving is simple and straightforward.
- Some people seem able to forgive quickly, but for many the process is "every day".
- Forgiving after trauma can be complex.
- Writing in a journal can be one way to try to make sense of our feelings.

Further reflections

- What is it we actually do when we forgive?
- What are the implications of "instant forgiving"?
- Are some things unforgivable?

CHAPTER 2

The Complications of Forgiveness

Integrity is very important to me ... I didn't feel I could celebrate the Eucharist, centred around peace, reconciliation and forgiveness as it is, when I feel so far from those things myself.

Revd Julie Nicholson, the *Daily Telegraph*, 7 March 2006

Someone whose daughter died on that horrendous day on 7 July 2005 was Julie Nicholson. She was a vicar in Bristol but resigned her post in March 2006 saying she couldn't forgive her daughter's killers. My first reaction on hearing this news was that it was far too early for her to be able to forgive. We were only eight months from that traumatic day. Who would she forgive, anyway? The bomber was dead. She'd had to bury her child – a nightmare scenario for any parent. Of course she would be struggling to forgive. I knew that if I were in her shoes and my daughter had died, I'd be in pieces.

It's impossible

But the more I heard Julie Nicholson talk on the radio and read her articles, the more I could see that she wasn't saying she was struggling to forgive – she was saying it was *impossible* for her to forgive. I was amazed at her bravery and her total honesty, and I think she has done something huge for everyone who finds "instant forgiving" so complex and difficult.

Anthony Bash, in his book *Just Forgiveness*, commenting on Julie Nicholson's difficulties, says:

> Surely, God does not ask of Ms. Nicholson – or any of the rest of us – something that, despite our best efforts, we find impossible? Would it not be a double blow if God were to withhold forgiveness from a victim because he or she has found it impossible to forgive?

Trying to define forgiveness

One interesting thing that arose as I read various books about forgiveness is that many writers try to define it, but end up saying it's almost too complicated to say what forgiving actually is. It's a verb – it means *what we actually do* when we forgive.

Given our uniqueness and that no two situations are identical, presumably when we try to "do forgiving" it is likely to be different in each individual circumstance; we are all likely to do it slightly differently.

Some writers say there are many kinds of forgiveness in which the complexities are an interwoven tangle of ideas, emotions, and spiritual longings. Anthony Bash, writing as a Christian theologian, says it is better to think of forgiveness**es** – lots of them – a collection of hugely varied activities that can be hard to define. That certainly fits with what I found as I read and talked to people during the research for this book.

- One obvious but overlooked aspect of forgiveness is that some awful events are very much harder to forgive than others.

- Sometimes forgiving is us responding to heartfelt apologies.

- Forgiving can include reconciliation – but it doesn't always; the relationship has sometimes broken down completely.

- Often there is no apology, putting the victim in a difficult position. They may even be told: "So I did it. Get over it." Some Christian theologians say that without an apology true forgiving can't happen, but we should instead talk about "letting go".

- Often hurt people do not get justice. Christian faith believes that "God is just" and yet, for example, for victims of abuse, justice is so often ignored.

A forgiveness framework

I found Anthony Bash's "forgiveness quintet" a good framework from which to start to understand forgiving. Bash says that to be "thick" forgiveness, a situation has to have these five features, and without all five, any forgiveness is "thin" and incomplete. (Some people believe that in those "thin" cases we shouldn't use the word "forgiveness", but perhaps say "letting go".) Here is my summary of his five points:

- It's a response to a wrongdoing – the victim makes the response and you can't forgive "by accident".

- Repentance from the perpetrator is crucial. (Hence many situations are "thin", and we may need to use a different word instead of "forgiveness".)

- Forgiveness is only about things that are morally wrong. Bash gives the example that if his friend wants to have a tattoo, he might suggest to his friend that might not be the best thing to do. But if the friend has the tattoo anyway, that's not morally wrong – it's a question of taste. (I like Bash's example because I have a tattoo of Eeyore on my leg!) Similarly, in situations of a genuine accident, that is not a moral wrongdoing.

- Often forgiveness involves restored relationships – but not always. In some situations renewing the relationship would not be appropriate.

- Justice must be seen as part of the meaning of forgiveness.

For there to be robust and true forgiveness – what Anthony Bash calls "thick" forgiveness – all five features of the quintet must be present, and this is an important point when considering the stories that follow in Section B of this book.

After that, and at the end of Section C, I will come back to trying to say more fully what forgiveness is, and what we actually do when we forgive.

Facing a difficult event

I began my thinking by talking to people who have been abused. As a survivor of childhood abuse myself, I was already in various groups where it was clear that Christian survivors were being "helped" by being told something along these lines:

"The sin here is not what was done to you but that you haven't forgiven yet."

In other words, any blame in the situation was being put on the victim, not the perpetrator of the crime.

Repeatedly, and surprisingly, I discovered Christian pastoral care was that ruthless – based on ignorance of the effects of trauma, of the forgiving process, and blatant rejection of the need for justice.

And this "blame" that is put back on the survivor adds to the huge amounts of guilt and shame that all survivors of abuse (both sexual abuse and other kinds of abuse) already seem to feel so deeply.

Research reports vary but the statistics are scary, indicating that abuse is much more prevalent than we might think.

- One in eight women and one in twelve men report that they were sexually abused before the age of sixteen.
- One in four girls and one in nine boys experience some kind of abuse in childhood.

I found on the web that most researchers were estimating that about one-fifth or maybe even a quarter of the adult population has been abused at some point in their life.

That's one in five or one in four people.

If we then add to that those who have struggled with some awful event such as:

- a hit and run accident
- a child killed by a drunk driver
- some kind of really serious mismanagement by a big organization such as the health services

we are talking about a huge percentage of the population for whom forgiving is likely to be far from straightforward – may, indeed, feel impossible, and in some circumstances may be inappropriate.

The joy and peace of forgiving

For some people, forgiving changes their life for the better. I heard a journalist being interviewed on the radio about her recovery from an awful event and she said that she had "forgiven her attacker". The interviewer asked her if this was from some religious standpoint. The journalist replied:

Oh, no. I'm not at all religious. But forgiving is so important – putting it all down. It's the only way to be.

This young journalist may not have religious beliefs, but she demonstrated a clear sense of her inner spirit and how to keep herself from negative resentments, and the inner chaos that can result from holding grudges.

People who forgive

When we think of the word "forgiveness", probably most of us can come up with someone who has forgiven in a way that has hit the headlines. The film *Singapore Story* tells of Bishop Leonard Wilson who was imprisoned by the Japanese in World War Two and tortured. His faith and willingness to forgive led to some of his captors converting to Christianity – such was the amazement at his generosity of spirit after such horrific treatment. Bishop Leonard later took a confirmation service for one of his captors.

When a gunman walked into an Amish school in America in October 2006 and shot ten young girls aged six to thirteen, then himself, the forgiveness of that Amish community was startling. What went around the world as news was the forgiveness; the newspapers in the UK were full of astonishment at the way that the Amish people turned in love to the family of the gunman, visiting and comforting the bereaved.

Finding freedom

There are numerous stories in which a victim forgives because of their Christian faith. My neighbour told me how her faith changed her relationship with her father. She found she was overreacting to some things and had quite a bit of inner turmoil, but was unable to work out why. One day, doing the washing-up, she realized she had never forgiven her father for molesting her when she was a teenager. She told me that as soon as she forgave him, she felt an inner peace and joy that was both overwhelming and amazing. She said she had forgiven her father in that moment, and that she had forgiven everything, and this led her into a closer relationship with God.

These kinds of stories show how forgiving can be healing and creative. It can release us from inner pain, help us to put down our grievances, and restore us to a happy and contented life.

Books about forgiving

But there can be a problem with the "instant and complete" forgiveness that some Christian counsellors and pastors recommend. As I've read my way through lots of books I found many have an attitude to forgiveness as the supreme way in which to live our lives. A part of me believes that to be true.

But, and it's a huge BUT, some people, including Christians who attempt to help others, seem to take "instant and complete" forgiveness to be *the only way to forgive* – a blueprint for everyone. And that can cause huge problems.

Some of these "instant and complete" forgiveness books use phrases such as:

- "We must be obedient to God's word which says we must forgive others."

- "Jesus commanded us from the cross to forgive so we must obey. It is the most important aspect of Christian life to forgive."

- "We must forgive or we will not be forgiven by God."

These books are full of emotive "shoulds" and "oughts" but interestingly, in some of these somewhat scary books there can be (but not always) a small section tucked in a corner acknowledging that sometimes forgiving isn't appropriate for some people in some circumstances.

This crucial thought is so buried within copious text that it gets lost! But it is this thought that is so important for those who struggle with forgiving.

This book is different

What I want to say in this book is that these "instant and complete" books give victims a very hard time. There's a clear sense of condemnation if you dare to admit you are struggling with forgiving. Some books say clearly that if you don't forgive, you will be shut out of God's kingdom; or, as one clergyman put it to me when I told him how hard I was finding it to forgive someone (I'd been attacked and was still trembling and having nightmares), "If you don't forgive, you will go to hell."

This is unjust, unhelpful, and plain wrong!

It seems to ignore the fact that some people have a heavy backpack of difficulties that they are trying to offload. They have been deeply hurt. They are trying to get their life back. They are weary of seeking justice and seeming to get nowhere. As Anthony Bash's book makes clear, it would be much more honest and do much less damage to already vulnerable people if Christian pastors, and indeed all of us, could recognize that even starting to consider forgiving can be extremely difficult.

Forgiveness can be terrifying

Of course forgiving is important, but in reality for many people – for example, those who have been traumatized – "forgiveness" can be a terrifying word that can bring overwhelming guilt, tears and that most dangerous of human conditions: despair. The next section contains some of their stories.

Key points

- The promise of "health, wealth and happiness around the corner" if we would "just forgive" can be inappropriate in many circumstances.
- It is difficult to define forgiving and easier to think of "forgivenesses".
- One framework of forgiving is the "forgiveness quintet".
- Forgiving can sometimes bring peace and contentment into shattered lives.
- For some, putting down the load of forgiving can be hugely difficult.

Further reflections

- In which kinds of circumstances can forgiving be inappropriate?

SECTION B

This section is a series of stories that demonstrate how some people picked up significant emotional burdens, and the responses from those around them.

There are many ways in which we can pick up burdens that weigh us down emotionally. Sometimes difficult events become so overwhelming that we collapse with a nervous breakdown, or go through a major depression, or experience debilitating anxiety.

Some of the stories open up the question of the relationship of justice with forgiveness; some illustrate the difficulty of deciding to forgive; some refer to "weird Christian thinking" that can get in the way of healing. Others illustrate the problems caused for those told they "must forgive" – even that they must "forgive and forget" – which can silence people who need to be listened to.

I shall use the image of "letting go" and "putting down burdens" and will explain these more fully as we go along.

It is the stories in this section that I will refer back to in Section C where I will try to tease out what forgiving actually is.

CHAPTER 3

Richard and Marion's Stories: A Difficult and Confusing Process

You must try harder. Jesus won't forgive you unless you forgive your parents.

(Max)

Richard had been abused by both his mother and his father from an early age. He couldn't remember a time when it wasn't happening, and his mother told him that masturbating him was the only way she could find to stop him crying when he was a baby. His parents were violent towards all their children, beating them, locking them in a cupboard and withdrawing food, sometimes for days.

Starting going to church

When Richard left home and went to art college in another town, he began to go to church because he felt lonely and depressed. Talking to the vicar one day, he told her how he felt and she said she had noticed how he was sometimes very angry during discussion groups. She offered Richard some free counselling from the church – there was a counselling service based in the old vicarage. Richard gratefully accepted that and asked for a male counsellor.

He had been seeing Max once a week for a few months and had established a good relationship with him. He'd been able to talk to Max about the sexual abuse and they were working on his anger, his depression and his sense of having been rejected by his parents.

Talking to parents

Max had supported Richard's decision to go home to talk to his parents about it. This conversation hadn't gone well and his parents had insisted they had done nothing wrong. Richard had hoped for an apology, but instead he felt even more upset and depressed, particularly because his mother had been manipulative and threatening. But things were going well with Max, and Richard began to trust him more and open up his deeply buried feelings.

But one day, Max seemed to change and their conversation went something like this:

Max: You will never get better, you know, unless you forgive your parents.

Richard: I do try to forgive them. I tell myself I am forgiving them, but then something happens and I feel so angry I know I haven't.

Max: Well, you will never get better unless you completely forgive them, so we need to work on that.

Richard: I really am trying to forgive.

Max: Well, you must try harder. Jesus won't forgive you unless you forgive your parents.

Richard: If only they'd said sorry.

Max: Well, they didn't say sorry, and if you don't want to go to hell, you must forgive them.

Richard said he was silent for a bit. He had never seen Max like this. Then he continued by saying that he wanted to forgive but it was really hard and he'd just end up feeling angry with his parents and also with himself.

Max quoted a Bible verse about not being angry and another one that he said showed "Jesus commanded us to forgive". Richard was devastated by Max's behaviour. All the past friendliness seemed to have disappeared. He tried to talk about this but Max kept to "you must forgive" and wouldn't say anything else for the whole session.

Richard went back to his room and cried for days. He couldn't bring himself to go back to see Max, nor could he go to the church again. He decided to abandon Christianity. He said: "The burden of all that guilt is just too hard to carry."

A common story

Marion's story is similar and I've included hers because, of all the stories people shared with me, what happened to Richard and Marion was by far the most common – a Christian counsellor or pastor says "You must forgive *now*" and chaos breaks out in the emotional life of a hurt person.

Marion told me how her vicar told her she must leave the church until she could forgive her father. Marion tried to explain that she was trying to do that, but she was struggling with forgiving and still felt angry and confused.

Marion told me how angry she was with her father. He had abused her as a child and he often beat up her mother. When Marion told her teacher what was going on, her father threw her out of the house. Years later her mother was dying and when Marion found this out, she longed to see her. But her father refused to let her. Understandably, Marion was very upset that her mother had died and she hadn't been allowed to hold her hand. She told her vicar about her distress but his response was only that Marion must forgive, or God wouldn't forgive her. He banned her from coming to Communion and any church service "until you can forgive".

Inappropriate responses

I find myself very angry about this kind of treatment because it seems to me not only to be completely inappropriate for any counsellor or pastor to have so little compassion, but I see it as working in direct opposition to what I read about the life of Jesus in the Bible. When I had two months study leave in America recently, I read all the four Gospels right through, and I see the man Jesus as loving, healing and compassionate.

So what has happened to love and compassion when people are told they must forgive or God won't forgive them?

Abused all over again

I had the privilege in America to be able to read in libraries and talk to people about forgiveness. David Augsburger, the author of many books on forgiveness, gave me some time and I cautiously told him Richard and Marion's stories. As I finished I said how often I had heard a very similar story. I looked into David's face wondering what his reaction would be. (He's a minister, family therapist, and hugely respected in the field of psychology as well as theology.) He looked at me and said, "Well, Sue, what those people have done is just to abuse those poor people all over again."

I was so relieved. I told him that much of my book will be about "weird Christian thinking" and we were able to talk through issues such as what people call Jesus' "commands" to forgive in the Lord's Prayer and in his words as he is crucified on the cross.

Yes, I would say that Richard, Marion and others who have a similar story were abused all over again. There is a lack of compassion, and a lack of reality. To have been abused by both parents must have done the most awful things to Richard's inner world as a child. How could he trust anyone if his primary caregivers abused him? How did he survive teenage years being sexually abused by his mother?

Devastating lives

Like many survivors of childhood abuse, Richard was eventually diagnosed with post-traumatic stress disorder. He spent some time in mental hospitals and found that on medication he became steadier and his nightmares and flashbacks became less upsetting.

He could see he would eventually be able to put down the burden of what his parents did to him, and make the best he could of his new life. He found it harder to forgive Max who had so broken his trust.

Marion left her church and found another community who welcomed and supported her, reassuring her that God loved her. She wept as she told me how relieved she felt. I could see how her burdens had been lifted.

Key points

- People who have experienced some horrific event can find forgiving a difficult and confusing process.
- But there is a widely held view that forgiving is easy.
- Some people believe that if we struggle to forgive, rather than being able to forgive instantly, God won't forgive us.
- Without an apology, forgiving is made much harder.
- We need to take care when talking to vulnerable people that we don't add to their burden with the words we use.

Further reflections

- If we feel angry, does that mean we have not forgiven, or started to forgive?
- How has the apparent lack of compassion illustrated in this chapter become so prevalent in some Christian circles?

CHAPTER 4

Jamie's Story: Weird Christian Thinking, and Striving for Justice

If Stan had apologized we would never have taken it to court.

(Jamie's grandmother)

Jamie was fifteen and on "suicide watch" because of serious bullying at school. Another boy known to the family had recently killed himself because he had been bullied, and Jamie was depressed and "not himself".

The youth club at church in a small town in Wales decided to raise money for charity by cleaning cars for the congregation, and others, one Saturday evening. Stan, a middle-aged man who came to church sometimes but had a drink problem, punched Jamie hard in the face in an unprovoked attack. No one else saw the incident and Stan denied doing it.

Jamie was deeply upset and badly hurt. He probably had felt quite safe with his mates cleaning cars – there would be no reason for him not to. Out of the blue he was both physically hurt and mentally rocked.

The family was in no doubt that the right thing to do was to call the police. Stan had broken the law. Assaulting someone is a crime, and it was also child abuse. Stan continued to deny doing it.

A surprising turn of events

A remarkable thing happened. The vicar of the church said that Jamie and his family should "just forgive Stan", adding that they should never have gone to the police and they should stop the case going to court. Many of the church fellowship and the wider local community agreed with the vicar. Just a few agreed with Jamie's family – few enough for the family to feel ostracized and almost guilty for what they were doing.

Stan continued to deny doing it.

Jamie was traumatized. He found going out of the house difficult. Going to school was now very hard for him. He didn't want to go to church. He was a very bright and able child, expected to go to university, but over the year before the court case his schoolwork deteriorated. He had nightmares. He was put on anti-depressants and the other three children in the family were inevitably drawn into the upset.

What could have happened?

"If Stan had apologized we would never have taken it to court," Jamie's grandmother told me. Yes, it could all have been very different. If Stan had owned up to what he did he might have been helped to see that he had a serious drink problem. He'd already been convicted of drink-driving, so to me it might have been very much more helpful if the vicar and the community got behind Stan and insisted that he go to Alcoholics Anonymous, or whatever was available in their town. That might have been the way to "love" Stan in this situation.

It would probably have been appropriate for Stan to make

reparation to Jamie and his family, perhaps by paying for Jamie's therapy and also for Jamie to have some kind of fun adventure holiday with his brother and sisters. That might have been an appropriate way to "love" Jamie in his situation.

Making some kind of reparation is very important when abuse has happened, particularly if the victim is a child or vulnerable adult. Jamie would inevitably meet Stan in the ordinary course of living. The boy needed a sincere apology so that he would feel safe – although he would be wise never to trust Stan.

Jamie's family said they knew things would have been totally different if Stan had apologized. They wouldn't have taken it to court – but they might well still want to have taken the matter to the police. That might have been a way to convince Stan to get the help he so obviously needed for his anger and drinking.

What did happen?

Stan refused to admit he had done anything wrong, and the case went to court. By this stage the church community was completely split, with some people very angry with Jamie's family. The vicar made it clear that the family was completely in the wrong and they felt unwelcome at church, despite having belonged there for almost forty years.

Stan's wife angrily told Jamie's grandmother that Stan might be sent to prison, and that it was the grandmother's fault! Stan's wife pointed out that she would have childcare problems because she would need to go out to work so that the family could afford to live. She was worried that Stan might lose his job and said "it's so unfair" and "it's your fault".

It's Jamie's family's fault?

No! The way to not go to prison is not to commit crime. If you don't want to lose your job, get a grip on your anger and drinking problem. Stan and his family, and the vicar, seemed to be in complete denial about the seriousness of Stan's problems – and the drinking got worse with the trial hanging over him.

Within the church and community, bizarrely, it was Stan who was seen as the wronged person and Jamie's family were seen as the wrongdoers. This weird situation is not uncommon when people take the "just forgive" attitude with absolutely nothing being done to prevent further wrongdoing by the perpetrator, and nothing done to help the victim to feel safe, valued, and supported.

It can be inappropriate to forgive

It's this kind of situation that demonstrates that there are times when "instant forgiving" can be inappropriate. It would allow Stan's drunken abusive behaviour to go on unchecked, so potentially he could wreck another life. Easy and quick forgiving causes problems.

The outcome

After the trial, in which Stan was found guilty, there was some time set aside for reports. During that phase Stan finally admitted that he had hit Jamie – which most people had known all along was the truth. He didn't go to prison, but tragically Jamie's parents split up.

Child abuse of any kind has a traumatic effect on everyone involved. For that family to feel rejected, isolated by their community, and particularly with the lack of support from the church, it was too much to bear. Anyone who is falsely accused of wrongdoing, as Jamie's family was, may well crack under the stress.

What was going on?

I've discussed this story many times with people as I researched this book. Ministers have said to me that they suspect the vicar was putting "peace at all costs" before the justice that Jamie deserved.

This story highlights the belief amongst Christians that "just forgive" is the way forward in all situations, and this is what I mean by "weird Christian thinking", because I think it distorts some of the central messages of Christianity. Over and over again I have seen this view of forgiveness cause considerable mental and spiritual anguish amongst people who turn to the church for help after they have experienced a painful event, only to meet with a lack of compassion and the view that "forgiving" is a kind of cure-all for every difficult situation.

Key points

- It's often the victims who are seen as in the wrong.
- Issues around forgiving can split communities.
- "Peace at all costs" is inappropriate when there are issues of justice.
- Wrongdoers need to take responsibility for what they do, and not necessarily expect just to be forgiven and no action taken.
- Making reparation as well as apologizing is important.

Further reflections

- Where has this bizarre thinking – "forgive everything even when it's inappropriate" – come from?

CHAPTER 5

Diana's Story: Forgiveness isn't a "Cure-all"

You must forgive your father.

(Diana)

Not long after Diana married Joe, he started to hit her. He would shout at her and make her do things she didn't want to – things relating to "ordinary" life but also to their sex life. Diana put up with it and tried to ignore it, but after one explosive outburst when she had several very obvious bruises on her face and body, she turned to her friend Alison for help. Because Joe was the church organist and choirmaster, Alison suggested Diana could tell the vicar. Diana found that a bit scary, but she thought she could talk to the vicar's wife, and ask her if she would tell the vicar.

Diana hadn't known what to expect. She was terrified of telling anyone because Joe had threatened her with beatings if she said anything. Both the vicar and his wife said that Diana's Christian duty was to forgive Joe, to "turn the other cheek", and to go back home and apologize for things she'd done to displease him. She was taken aback by this because she couldn't think what she'd done wrong, but she did as they suggested.

A listening friend

Alison, not a churchgoer, was horrified at this advice and told Diana to tell the police about Joe and to get out of the house. Diana knew this sounded the right thing to do, but because she was a Christian, she thought she should forgive him as she had been told.

A few years later, Diana gave birth to twins, a boy and a girl. Joe was delighted, but in the first few weeks of looking after two newborn babies he became stressed, and he and Diana lacked sleep. He began to hit her again. He wouldn't help with night feeds and he planned a big Christmas concert with the choir so was out several evenings, leaving her alone with the babies.

Diana became depressed. She felt abandoned and couldn't cope with the babies, and Joe became even more violent. She went to see the new vicar and was told to go back home and support Joe in his work for the church, forgive him, and get on with being a wife and mother.

Forgive and forget

The violence went on for over twenty years. All the advice Diana had from Christian friends was to forgive and forget. As far as she was aware, no one challenged Joe about his abusive behaviour. It was only Alison who was telling Diana to get out and get help. She came to help Diana with the babies in their early years, but then moved away from the area.

You must forgive

Sometimes Joe was physically abusive to his children, and hit Diana in front of them. Diana always told her children they must forgive their father. But when the twins were away at university, some young adults who had been in the choir disclosed that Joe had sexually abused them when they were younger – both boys and girls. When the twins heard about this they too disclosed that their father had sexually abused them. They had realized as children that he did it to both of them, but they were too frightened by his threats to say anything. He told them no one would believe them, and their mother would know it was their fault and they would be sent to live in a children's home.

Diana's guilt

Naturally Diana was devastated at what her children had gone through without her knowing. She split up from Joe and felt desperately guilty, wondering if her children would blame her for not noticing their father abusing them – but they didn't. The three of them began to get some family therapy and Diana became aware of how angry she felt that the advice she had been given was all about her going back and forgiving Joe. She realized that if she'd followed her gut feeling from the start and followed her friend Alison's advice, the twins might never have been sexually abused by Joe.

Diana told me that she regretted telling her children when they were young that they must forgive their father. She said she thought it was the right thing to do at the time but now realized that it was totally inappropriate.

Both her son and daughter had been deeply hurt. They both rejected Christianity, the girl saying that she couldn't deal with anything that had a "father"; she certainly didn't want a "heavenly Father". But they both agreed that now the truth was out in the open they were beginning to feel better. The therapy was helping them and Diana to get their lives back.

Head in the sand

Here again, just like Jamie's story, we see some Christians with weird thinking. How could it possibly have been right to tell Diana to go back to a violent partner and not (apparently) do anything about her or her children's safety? It looked as if no one helped Joe to change his behaviour, perhaps by talking with him about whatever was making him so angry and violent.

This is a very strange kind of denial – a refusal to see a potentially life-threatening situation. (More murders than we might think are committed by partners.) Hopefully these days we are all a little more alert about keeping children safe – but I know from things people have told me that this kind of situation is still going on today. Domestic violence is still a huge problem, and children go on being abused by relatives and "friends".

Forgiving a cure-all?

This is another story where forgiveness is seen as the "cure" for everything. Any sense of reparation, justice, and ordinary human common sense and love for a neighbour seems to get totally abandoned in this attempt to promote forgiveness as some kind of supreme way of solving all problems.

Diana and her children deserved justice. But more than that, they deserved some kind of love and protection from those around them – some kind of social concern, Christians caring for her, responding to the clear needs of a mother and her children. They deserved some kind of reality check about what was really happening, not this head in the sand attitude that "all will be well if you would only forgive".

Key points

- Those who are addicted to anger, violence and abuse need help in order to learn to change their behaviour.
- Diana and her children deserved justice, and to be protected.
- It is when the truth of a situation comes out that healing can begin.

Further reflections

- When some kind of painful event has happened, it is important to explore the link between forgiving and justice.
- In situations of domestic abuse it is crucial to protect the victim and children.

CHAPTER 6

John's Story: Forgive Now, or You're Doomed

Forgiveness comes at the end of the healing process. It isn't how we start. There is a great deal to do and to understand before we can forgive with any meaning.

(A psychotherapist)

John's early life was awful. He lived with horrific physical and sexual abuse from his parents and older brother. He was in his twenties when I met him. He had recently become a Christian and he had been told he must forgive, or God wouldn't forgive him.

I tried to soften this over the few days I was with him and some others at a healing week for survivors of abuse. I was trying not to intrude into John's life too much, but I was horrified how often John said, "I must forgive or God won't forgive me." He didn't actually say much else the whole week.

John would agree that he believed God loved him, and then he would say, "But God won't forgive me unless I forgive them. That's what my pastor at church says."

A huge burden

As we were all leaving to go home, I once again assured John that God's love for him would never end – ever – whether he was angry with his family for what they did to him, or if he was finding it hard to forgive them. I said that forgiving is hard, but it would come to him as he gradually worked through his issues. God would never reject him.

John nodded, and then said, "But God won't forgive me if I don't forgive them." It was almost as if he had a mantra that he couldn't break away from, and as John was taken home by the pastor from his church, I wondered what Jesus would have said to that lovely young man. I suspect he might have hugged John and told him how much he loved him. I really don't think he'd be wagging his finger at him in disapproval and telling him he'd better get a grip on himself otherwise he's out there on his own.

The good news

The story of Jesus is said to be "good news". This good news is about the unconditional love of a Great Creator. It isn't about a God who wags his finger at us and tells us, "That's it. I don't love you any more. Goodbye." But that is how John perceived it – because of the teaching by his pastor.

As I'll discuss in Section C, there are some parts of the Bible that can be hard to understand, but the main theme is abundantly clear: the love of a Creator God who made us and will love us to the end. It's like those sticks of peppermint rock that say "Brighton" all the way through. The Bible says "God's unconditional love for everyone" all the way through.

A tragedy

The tragedy of John's life during that week I was with him was that he only seemed to be able to focus on his need to forgive. My perception of him was that he needed instead to focus on God's welcoming love, and his own healing. I know from my own experience of healing that as we heal our emotional wounds, so forgiveness and "putting down our burdens" gradually becomes easier. Having been pushed into inappropriate forgiving myself by some people, I felt so sorry for John.

Many of the people on that week talked about their healing. For me it was a thrilling journey into turning the nightmares in my head into creativity and peace. I came home aware of so much inner healing, but sadly, I don't think John experienced that.

Healing comes first

As so many people have said to me over the past few years, forgiveness comes as we work at our healing. It isn't necessarily what we do first (but of course the intention to forgive could come early in the healing process). It's the healing that usually comes first, and as one of my wonderful psychotherapists pointed out to me when I'd been pushed towards forgiving by someone, "Sue, you don't yet know what it is that you have to forgive."

We need to know what it is that we have to forgive before we can forgive with any meaning.

Key points

- Forgiving is part of our healing process, but we may need to experience considerable healing before we know what we actually need to forgive.

- Forgiving is more likely to grow as we start to heal emotionally and come to terms with what has happened to us. It is less likely to be the first thing we need to do – although it is for some.

- Hurt people need to hear about love, not about threats.

- It is unhelpful – possibly even damaging – to pressurize people into forgiving.

CHAPTER 7

My Mother's Story: Hatred Going Down the Generations

It can be easier to forgive an enemy than friends and family.

(A psychologist)

One of the points often made in books about forgiving is that it is always much harder to get a grip on forgiveness when it involves someone in our family, and this definitely rings true for me and my birth family. No one ever apologized. There would be huge violent rows – then silence. Once the last broken plate was swept up and in the bin, it was as if all the anger went in the bin too.

But it lurked there within our house, waiting to leap out and engulf us.

Although my stepfather was a really violent person, as I grew older I realized how much my mother provoked him, and was full of anger, bitterness and hatred of a whole range of things.

As a Scot, she loathed and despised the English. As we travelled on holiday in Scotland over the years I found out that her hatred was mainly about the Battle of Culloden, when the English soldiers slaughtered the Scots. To me as a child this seemed a pretty good reason for being cross, but when I discovered that this battle had been 200 years before I was born, I wondered how my mother could still be so resentful.

It seemed to me also to be dangerous to go on about it as we drove through the Scottish glens with my English stepfather's neck gradually changing from pale pink to purple as his silent anger grew.

My mother's rages about the savagery of the English always led to retaliation; if not that evening in some hotel, or in the homes of some surprised cousins, it would come up months later as they tore each other apart after a night of drinking.

Mothers and daughters

It wasn't until I had two children of my own, the second one a daughter, that my mother revealed to me the basis of another of her own twisted hatreds. I had tried so very hard to love her – and as a young person I'm sure I did love her, though I found her manipulative and incredibly inconsistent as I grew older. She seemed a very complicated person to understand. At times she seemed to hate me, but at other times could be quite caring.

We were sitting in the garden of a mental hospital where I was attempting to recover from post-natal depression following my daughter Rachel's birth, and she said something along these lines:

> Of course, you won't get on with Rachel and she won't get on with you. It's like that in our family. Mothers and daughters just don't get on. You've never got on with me and I don't get on with you. My mother hated me and I hated her. What a bitch she was. She hated her mother and her mother hated her, and so on.

I was absolutely astonished. Did I really not get on with my mother? It was all completely extraordinary because I thought I got on with her well enough. I forget what I said in reply to my mother; my inner world was working overtime. I remember writing in my journal to God something along these lines:

> OK, God, this is your big moment. If all that stuff about you giving us a Holy Spirit to help us through life is true, I really need some of that strength now. I will never, ever allow myself not to get on with my precious daughter. Please help me to break this awful chain of bitterness that has gone on down the generations in my family. Please help me to go on loving my baby just as passionately as I do now. Help us to grow into good friends. Did you hear me, God?

God did hear me. I am hugely proud of my amazing daughter, and I love her even more passionately than I thought could be possible. She's such a good friend. She now has three little daughters of her own, and I know with certainty that all that baggage that weighed me and my mother's family down is long gone – and will not be there in the lives of my grandchildren.

Years later, as I sat with my mother in the few months as she lay dying, I came to see more clearly what an unhappy person she was. I knew this as a child, of course, but as an adult I was able to see how her many resentments and hatreds contributed to that sadness.

Key points

- Burdens of bitter and twisted hatred that exist in families, countries and tribes can negatively influence families and communities.
- Hatred that clings on over the generations can be very difficult to heal. But it can be transformed: it does not have to be passed on.

Further reflections

- The different strands of forgiveness can be difficult to untangle, but forgiving is almost always about relationships, love and communities.

CHAPTER 8

Attacked: Dealing with Outrage and Seeking Justice

Forgiveness is not to be confused with a martyrish passivity. Forgiveness may only be possible after the victim's outrage has spurred action to ensure that there are structural impediments against future abuse.

(Fraser Watts, Rebecca Nye and Sara Savage)

Some years ago I was out walking my dog when I was verbally and physically attacked by a couple of people we vaguely knew. It seems they had some sort of long-standing grudge against me, or against my husband, David (or perhaps it was against the church that David works for). The things they said were horrible and unrepeatable, and although the woman's punches and slaps weren't particularly hard, I was deeply shocked and my body was trembling. They threatened me – "We will get you!" – and all I could think about was getting my little dog away from them. She was terrified.

I found the whole experience traumatic, probably because it reawakened in me the abuse from my childhood, and I began to feel very unsafe. Even as the attack was happening, I was telling myself that I would need to forgive these people, but in fact it took me a very long time to find a way to put down the burdens of what happened.

Don't tell the police

What made the situation worse for me was that though I was keen to go to the police, church friends urged me not to. They said that it would "bring disrespect to the church". Before a week had gone by I realized this advice was completely wrong.

As David said a few weeks after the attack, "the church thing" was at the back of my emotional distress and at the time I felt abandoned and badly treated by the church.

I found I couldn't live in our house any more because I couldn't sleep. I lived in permanent anxiety, my heart pounding all day. I had terrible nightmares, and not feeling safe, I just cried a lot of the time. In terms of the quote from Fraser Watts at the start of this chapter, it did not feel that there was anything in place that was going to protect me against future abuse, since the couple lived nearby.

No justice

I'm now sure that if I'd followed my own instinct and phoned the police straight away and had their involvement, I'd have recovered more quickly from the attack, because presumably they would have done what police do in these kinds of circumstances – told the couple off or whatever, and I'd have had at least some sense of justice. But for me, weeks later, the whole incident still hadn't "ended" in my inner world. Without the police involvement, they completely got away with what they did, and I believed that might leave them feeling they could repeat their crime when they chose to.

Eventually I did ring the police, but I didn't tell them who the attackers were. I was by that stage terrified the couple would hurt me even more if I reported them. But it was hugely comforting to get a crime number, and to talk the incident through with a woman police officer. She thought it was "stupid" to have been told not to tell the police because she could have sorted it out on the day it happened.

The policewoman said there had been two crimes.

- They had threatened me with further violence – "We'll get you!"

- Hitting me was an "assault".

She told me she was proud of me for not retaliating, and this was hugely comforting at the time.

Overwhelming emotions

Without a sense of safety, my mental health deteriorated, until I ended up feeling suicidal, which shocked me deeply. I thought I'd left all that behind long ago during earlier deep depressions. But it was the return of the death wish that shook me – and that in a sense drove me into learning how to put down those overwhelming burdens of fear, hopelessness and sheer terror.

So it was at this point that I began monitoring my emotions carefully.

- Why was I getting worse not better?

- How could I get myself out of this sense that I was carrying a huge burden that was weighing me down and destroying my life?

- What would forgiveness mean in practice, and why was the forgiving process so painful?

As I began writing in my journal, I could see that I'd been trying to hold down my emotions, probably because they were so scary. I realized I was imagining the couple coming to attack me again. At the time this felt terrifyingly real, but as I look back on it now, I see this was an unlikely scenario – but it was that same fear I'd had since childhood of unpredictable violence breaking out; a common feature of my family life when I was small.

Our response to trauma

I could see that some people might well have reacted to a similar attack very differently from me. Some might have been able to brush it off and resume normal life, but because I'd experienced so much trauma as a child, my inner world had gone into chaos. And one outcome of that was that I was struggling with forgiving these people, despite wanting to, and despite thinking that I had to (as I thought at the time) if I was to get back to some stability in my life.

Acknowledging our true emotions

It was only as I began to paint my emotions that I realized how deep my inner anger was. From then on I let myself paint my rage onto huge bits of paper with black paint and thick brushes. I forced myself to write about it in my journal, letting my true emotions have a chance to come out. I was a bit shocked at how angry I was. I even wanted revenge! I had no idea I had been thinking that. I was able to reject it. But it led me to read the book *Getting Even: Forgiveness and its Limits* by Jeffrie G. Murphy, which was very helpful.

Once I gave myself permission to listen to my inner world, rather than just pretending I was OK, I understood what was weighing me down. I was angry with this couple, but even more furious with those who had told me not to tell the police.

I had been trying to be calm and mature about the whole situation, shrugging it off, whereas it was only when I acknowledged that I was full of rage that I began to feel a sense of inner healing.

The stages of forgiving

Once I'd clarified to myself what was going on in my inner world, I set off on a healing journey that took many months. I was considerably helped by a loving and sensible Christian friend. I continued to write about my recovery. I could see that there were some stages I moved through – and even now as I write this I find my heart racing and my breathing changing. I decided I wanted to forgive the couple years ago, and as far as I can understand it, I think I have forgiven them, but it has been an ongoing process. There are still scars, and I often have to remind myself that when the event pops into my mind, it's best to "let go" of the mental image of being attacked completely out of the blue, and remind myself that the situation has ended.

I still wish I'd got justice! But working through the forgiving process has been very significant for me in the process of writing this book.

Key points

- Some people are likely to find forgiving easier than others because of early life experiences. For example, earlier trauma can be reawakened, prolonging the forgiving process.

- If a crime is reported there is a greater chance of victims getting justice, of the perpetrators being stopped from repeating their crime; this can help the victim to start on the healing process.

- Forgiving is a process which can have stages.

- Forgiving when there is an institution, organization or other "big system" involved can be complex because there is often no one person who carries the responsibility for what went wrong, or no one person who can make a decision to help the victim to start to recover.

- Recognizing what we are really feeling can be an important part of the healing and forgiving process.

Further reflections

- Our responses to traumatic situations will vary according to the "attachment" we formed as a child with our primary caregiver/s. More about this in chapter 21.

CHAPTER 9

Louise and Her Children are Abandoned: The Relationship Between Forgiving and Getting an Apology

---

We are too angry to forgive.

(Friends of Louise)

One day, Bob just walked out on his wife Louise and four children. He gave no reason. He refused to engage in any kind of counselling. He refused his wife's pleas to try to work at things that might be wrong in their marriage. He refused to pay a penny towards the upkeep of the house and children and went to live in Australia, where he "disappeared".

Louise was devastated. She felt that they had been reasonably happy, though she admitted that there were a few things they needed to work on in their relationship. But nothing had given her any reason to suspect that Bob was ready to leave her and abandon his children.

Children are grieving

The children grieved for their father. They adored him and loved him for the way he played with them, took them camping and swimming, and supported them in doing their homework. They'd had no idea he was unhappy, so for them and their mother, the shock was profound.

The oldest child got a place at an Ivy League college in the USA, so Louise tried to find Bob because she hoped he might be so proud of his son that he would support him financially. Louise was always short of money now because Bob had been the main breadwinner, but when Bob was eventually located, he refused to help with the money – then disappeared again.

Louise was confused because as a Christian she thought she should forgive Bob, but she found that extraordinarily difficult.

Can I forgive?

Louise and Bob had been active church members, so it was a shock to the whole community. Louise felt a huge burden of guilt. What was it she had done, or not done, to drive Bob away? Why would he not even talk about it all and say what his problem was? How could he cut himself off from everything, so suddenly and unexpectedly?

Church members told her she must forgive, but Louise found the whole situation a challenge to her faith. Did God really want her to forgive this man who had abandoned his children, seeming not to care about their daily tears?

Louise knew she was going to struggle with the upkeep of a big house and garden, but she wanted to keep the children in as stable an environment as she could. She felt trapped and, not surprisingly, a few months later she became depressed and anxious. Because money was so tight she stopped eating so that she could feed her children, resulting in her becoming anorexic.

Friends help

Louise joined a group of people who had experienced depression where she found support and friendship, and most people thought that she need not forgive Bob. He hadn't apologized. He hadn't made any attempt to put right what he had done. He never gave a penny to Louise for the children.

Eventually Louise felt that she could let go, or put down the burden of guilt and sadness that she was feeling. She did this for her own mental health and her depression lifted. Even years later she acknowledged that she thought it inappropriate to forgive Bob in her circumstances. She said: "I'm leaving the forgiving to God."

Please forgive me

One odd aspect of the story was that Bob wrote to some friends and asked them to forgive him for walking out of their life. These friends had been trying to support Louise and the children, so were puzzled about how to respond to Bob. Even if they could forgive him for what he had done to them, how could they forgive him for what he had done to Louise? They were furious with him for walking out on her, but recognized that he hadn't actually wronged them. When Louise wrote to the address on Bob's letter, she got no response.

The friends felt they were not in a position to forgive Bob, but wondered whether as Christians they should forgive him. But their anger was so great that it felt all wrong to tell him they had forgiven him. What could any kind of forgiveness mean in this kind of situation? What Bob needed to do was make some kind of reparation.

Bob was a Christian and they were confused about why he suddenly did something that seemed so selfish.

No right answer

They puzzled about what to do. Did Bob need their support, so should they respond positively to him? Should they tell him how angry they were at what he had done to Louise, or would that just drive him away further so they might lose all contact with him? If they wrote and forgave him, might that mean that he would eventually want to come back to his family? Or would doing so be untruthful to their real feelings? Should they keep some kind of contact for Louise's sake? And Bob was godfather to one of their children, so should they keep contact for the sake of their child?

There was no right answer. The situation was too complex for that and even years later Louise said it wasn't appropriate for her to forgive Bob because he never contacted them. He never even sent his children birthday cards, and their sense of being abandoned and rejected severely influenced their lives.

Key ideas

- Forgiving can be complex and confusing.
- Being rejected and abandoned can create a massive emotional burden for both adults and children.
- In circumstances where we think forgiving is inappropriate we can still put the burden down for our own mental health and "leave the forgiving to God".

Further reflections

- How important is some kind of apology for forgiveness to be offered?
- It's important to consider the effects on a person if they know they are not forgiven, especially when they have asked for forgiveness.
- What is the role of reparation in situations of hurt and abandonment?

CHAPTER 10

Lizzie and the Sex Offender: More Weird Christian Thinking

I know I'm a wicked and worthless person and I can never forgive myself for being like that. I'm a terrible person and suppose I deserve all the mental pain I go through.

(Lizzie)

I got to know Lizzie when I was leading a seminar about depression. She was very sad and anxious, and told me her story of childhood sexual abuse and rejection by her family. She was taken into care at twelve and had a few experiences of being fostered in families where again she was sexually abused.

Despite this chaotic childhood, Lizzie got a degree and then went on to train as a social worker. Because she was still experiencing some flashbacks and difficulties because of the childhood trauma she only worked part-time but managed to stabilize her life.

Becoming a social worker

Lizzie became a Christian at university, and when she got her job as a social worker, she found a church nearby where she put down some roots. She said she found the vicar of the church

73

quite challenging because she perceived him as bossy and overwhelming, but she made an approach to him with the report on sexual abuse by Churches Together in Britain and Ireland called *Time for Action*. She asked the vicar if they could study the report as a church, to which he said:

> We don't have any survivors of abuse in our church and we definitely have no abusers, so there wouldn't be much point given all the other things there are to do.

Lizzie found his response extraordinary – and upsetting – but she so enjoyed the house group she'd been part of for a few years that she decided she wouldn't pursue the matter with the vicar.

The house group was hosted by a young couple whom she found supportive and friendly. She spent five years in the group; she said her faith developed and she was healing well – she experienced fewer flashbacks and she found she was less phobic about loud noise, being near men, and having to be in a crowd.

A sex offender

But then the vicar told the congregation that a sex offender, Jason, wanted to join the church. He explained they were to forgive him and rejoice that in prison Jason had become a Christian. Lizzie told me that after her initial surprise she was quite happy about this new member of the congregation, but more and more she was finding the vicar overwhelming. She said he seemed unaware that he abused his position of power over people so she only went to the early morning Communion service because this was usually quiet and gentle. Some others in the congregation were fed up with having such a controlling vicar.

You must forgive him

A few weeks after Jason joined the church, the young couple at the house group said that Jason wanted to join their group. Lizzie was distraught and asked if he could go to one of the other seven groups because she would feel uncomfortable with him in such an intimate meeting in a relatively small room.

She was shocked to discover that this resulted in a barrage of blame from the young couple and the vicar. "You must forgive him," they all said to Lizzie, and she explained that she didn't see what it was she had to forgive. He hadn't done anything to her, but she wouldn't feel safe in "her" house group.

An unforgiving attitude?

Lizzie was particularly shocked and upset that the young couple seemed to be rejecting her. She had explained some of her background privately to them and at the time they had seemed to understand. But now they were telling her that if she didn't forgive Jason and manage to cope with him in the house group, she would find herself outside the love of God because of her unforgiving attitude.

A few weeks went past during which time Lizzie tried to explain her feelings to people in the house group and at church. She couldn't see why Jason couldn't go to one of the other house groups. In one discussion with the vicar she couldn't cope with his bullying attitude and she ran out of the meeting, confused and upset.

"Repent of your unforgiveness"

The vicar followed the meeting up with a letter in which he said that if Lizzie couldn't forgive Jason she would have to leave the house group, she would not be welcome at church and he would refuse to give her Communion until she could "repent of her unforgiveness".

This was all too much for Lizzie, and over the next few weeks and months she found herself isolated and friendless. The house group members all agreed with the vicar and in her loneliness she became depressed and began experiencing more flashbacks. After a few months she found she was unable to keep working and her mental state deteriorated. She started to self-harm by cutting herself – something she hadn't done since she was a teenager in care.

Lizzie told me that she felt she was "a wicked and worthless person" and said: "I can't forgive myself."

Abusive treatment by the church

Lizzie had to move from her flat because she couldn't afford the rent and what started out as cutting down on food because she didn't have much money resulted in her becoming anorexic.

Her doctor arranged some counselling for her at the GP practice and she developed a good relationship with her counsellor, Eve – who confirmed for Lizzie that "forgiving Jason" was a "ridiculous" idea. Eve was appalled at Lizzie's abusive treatment by her church and encouraged her to join a therapy support group for people with eating problems.

"I thought I was such a terrible person"

When I met Lizzie she was still depressed and unable to work. She'd joined another church with people whom she found loving and supportive, and the woman vicar said she'd see Lizzie once a fortnight to "sort out the whole forgiveness thing". These meetings were helpful as Lizzie explored what forgiving really meant. "I thought I was such a terrible person because I couldn't forgive the bloke [Jason], but it didn't make any sense," she said. "But Nancy [the vicar] said the other church were 'mad' even to consider forgiving Jason." He hadn't wronged them. What they needed to do was love Jason and accept him – but they most certainly should never trust him!

Key points

- Integrating a sex offender into a church requires very careful thought and establishing boundaries with the offender.
- Forgiving is quite different from the more appropriate "accepting" of a sex offender.
- The church's rejection of a survivor could have long-term consequences for the survivor in terms of loss of trust.

Further reflections

- Sometimes this weird thinking amongst Christians about forgiving can lead to damaging people, and give a very negative picture of the church and its pastoral response to vulnerable people.

CHAPTER 11

Everyday Forgiving: Problems in Ongoing Relationships

The most creative power given to the human spirit is the power to heal the wounds of the past it cannot change.

(Lewis Smedes)

The stories so far in this section have all been about significant events that have changed people's lives, but I felt that there is another story that is very important: the "everyday" one – the one most people face in the course of their lives.

- The family member who always puts us down.
- The abusive parents.
- The boss at work who seems to be intent on making our life difficult.
- The "friend" who is in the habit of taking out their own frustrations on us and is becoming increasingly unpleasant and manipulative.
- The neighbour who plays loud music and is abusive when we ask her to turn it down.

Ongoing problems

If we are in these kinds of situations there is likely to be an ongoing problem with managing being treated badly, and the resulting burden of feelings that verbal abuse (or whatever the problem is) brings – frustration, anger, guilt, shame, resentment, and so on.

Often we are left having to cope with the burdens that being treated inappropriately give us, and because it is an ongoing problem, not just an event in the past (though almost always terrible events in the past can be part of the problem), trying to put down this daily burden needs a great deal of courage – and considerable personal strength.

In these kinds of ongoing situations, where there is no apology and no attempt to treat us any better, "letting go" or "putting down our burden" might be a better way to think about the situation than "forgiving". If we want to think of ourselves forgiving, it is a clear illustration of what Gee Walker said:

[Forgiving is] every day... oh... every day.

Freezing

However much we might be able to "forgive" the person who is constantly mistreating us, because we have to go on meeting them, we're walking, maybe every day, into a situation that will inevitably provoke upsetting feelings in us. Obviously at times this can become raging resentment. I think that's a normal reaction – but it can create chaos in our mind if we think we are trying to forgive.

Another way to deal with ongoing abuse is to "freeze". I learned to do this as a child, although it's something I'm usually not all that aware of doing; it just happens. It's the missing aspect of what I learned in biology at school when I was taught that in a stressful situation we do one of two things: "fight or flight". I think there's a third response, "freezing", and for me this was the beginning of me dissociating – cutting myself off and living in a "dream world". In this alternative universe I felt safe. It was such a great place to be and I think it was the key to my survival as a child.

But I don't think that it's a particularly healthy thing to do. I more or less grew out of the involuntary dissociating, but many people continue to live with considerable amounts of dissociating in their lives. It's not in any way "wrong" – for many it's an important way of dealing with difficult issues in their life, and the dissociating is not always in their control.

When I was researching my book about healing from abuse, I came to see that dissociating can be very different for each individual.

There is also a healthy dissociating that I do as I run. I can switch off and be "somewhere else in my head" as I run beside the River Thames enjoying the birds singing and the wind in the trees. These are times I feel particularly close to God.

But dissociating in order to survive can, I think, link with some difficulties with forgiving, because we aren't always in touch with reality and it can involve issues of "limbic lag" that I discuss in chapter 23.

Something has to change

Even if we can find a way to tolerate our ongoing treatment by a person or organization, and maybe even manage to put down the burden of resentment quickly and efficiently, if you're anything like me, the ongoing situation becomes increasingly exhausting and we can become mentally and spiritually drained, as if our backpack is now bigger than us and we're starting to crack under the strain.

It might take us decades to get to the point where we realize something has to change because our body is so efficient at getting us to freeze – and one outcome of this is we forget what has happened. This is common in childhood sexual abuse; victims often "forget" what happened until something triggers a memory years later.

What we can't usually change

If we are in an ongoing awful situation we can't change other people. That is one of the known facts about relationships, but surprisingly many people set out to change others. Disaster! It isn't going to work. Well, not usually, anyway. There was no chance of changing my mother as I trekked across London twice a week for months as she lay dying of cancer. I was never going to be good enough for her and she would announce most weeks that the only one of her children she ever loved was my older half-brother. I couldn't change my mother. I could only change myself and my attitude to the situation, and my way of dealing with the relentlessness of it was to pray lots and just keep on driving – gritting my teeth and smiling at my mother no matter what she threw at me.

Attempting some kind of change

Some things are easy to change, such as buying wax earplugs to cope with a neighbour's noisy radio, but ongoing difficult relationships are difficult to change and can be personally costly.

A relationship in which we are repeatedly put down or bullied can tend to make us feel we deserve no better. That is our low self-esteem making us feel that we are so utterly hopeless that we can't do anything about our situation, and we tend just to give in and go along with it as well as we can. Any kind of change is likely to feel unsafe and maybe impossible.

This is "doormat syndrome". We may feel so powerless that all we can do is let people walk all over us – and this isn't healthy. Standing up for justice can often feel impossible. (There is more about "doormat syndrome" in chapter 15.)

Do we dare ask for justice?

A big problem with ongoing difficult relationships is that it's far easier (at one level) to go on putting up with it. (Lots of children in abusive homes do this. Mostly they have little choice and are dependent on other adults intervening on their behalf.)

Part of my story is that as my self-esteem developed I'd entered new territory (through working at recovering from childhood abuse). I now realize that I don't have to put up with being treated badly by people.

Dumpers and sorters

I have a "difficult friend" who used to dump some of her emotional baggage on me. It was another friend, Fran, who helped me to see that this "difficult friend" was a "dumper", and that was leaving me feeling overwhelmed and overburdened, partly because I am a "sorter" and like things in my life to make sense.

"It's her stuff," Fran pointed out, and as the years and months went by, I wondered if I might write to my friend, apologizing for my part in what I called the "difficulties in our relationship", and explaining what I was struggling with. But how could I do that without hurting her? How could I find the courage to say something to someone so aggressive that I was scared of her?

What am I changing?

If we say anything along the lines of "you really hurt me when you said/did that", there's a chance we might get, "Oh, I'm so sorry." But going from things people have told me when they have tried to "say something", we also need to be ready for some kind of explosion or a complete breakdown of the relationship for years – maybe even for ever.

Being selfish?

We also need to be aware that some people will say that we shouldn't speak out and ask to be treated better – some might even say that searching for justice and better treatment for yourself is selfish.

I can see that in some circumstances, when we are dealing with someone who is vulnerable and maybe weaker than us, it can be best to keep silent. That was how I treated my mother. There seemed no point at all in making her already sad life any worse by me bleating about her cruel behaviour towards me.

But I think every human being deserves to be treated with respect and dignity and not to have their spiritual and emotional boundaries invaded. It's part of "loving our neighbour as ourselves" – a crucial cornerstone of civilization as I know it – and being in a "toxic" relationship is damaging for everyone involved.

Forgiving?

One of the interesting things I've noticed about the ongoing difficult relationships I've been in is that unless I change what is going on by saying, "I'd like to be treated more kindly", it's likely that the bad treatment will just go on and on. So what is the place of any kind of forgiveness in this?

- Maybe the person who is treating us badly isn't aware of the effects they have on us.
- Maybe they have so little self-awareness that they don't think much about the effects of what they do and say on people.
- Maybe they've got so used to us being a "doormat" that they go on putting us down, to the point where it might give them a personal boost to see us cowed and frightened.

In none of these kinds of situations is the person likely to say to us one day, "I'm so sorry that for years I've been so abusive towards you."

Well, I suppose someone might say that if they are working hard to make their own life better. But mostly I think we aren't going to get an apology while the relationship remains as it has been.

"Forgiving" in these everyday stories can seem just as complicated as in the traumatic ones. It's difficult – and risky. And so much easier to leave the situation as it is! Maybe all we can do in these circumstances is "let go" as well as we can.

Not demonizing

One thing that can help us to forgive, or "let go" of bad treatment is to make sure we don't demonize the person. For example, my mother was a very damaged person, and so focused on her own life that I don't think she was aware of how upsetting I found it to face her constant criticisms.

I'm not meaning so much that we must excuse bad behaviour – "Oh dear, she had such a bad life!" – but rather remembering that all people we encounter struggle with the same human condition that we do. All of us know what we mean by "good" and "evil" and we can sometimes create idealized perceptions of people; we can say of one, "she is good", and say of another, "she is evil". But if we interpret them entirely like this – for example, me seeing the people who attacked me as entirely evil – we are heading off in the wrong direction.

Forgiveness, or "letting go" if that feels more appropriate in our situation, is another way of saying that none of us are completely good or completely evil, but all of us are capable of good and bad. None of us are angels or devils. Forgiving breaks down these idealizations and it is that act of letting go that can free us from clinging onto burdens that weigh us down.

Key points

- Most of us face day-to-day difficulties and irritations that can have a significant influence on our life.

- We cannot change other people.

- It is us, and our attitudes, that need to change first.

- Self-understanding is a crucial factor for good communication with others.

- We need to stop ourselves demonizing others.

Further reflection

- How are we going to find strategies to help us to let go and cope in difficult ongoing situations? (This is discussed in chapter 27.)

SECTION C

The key themes that emerge from stories in the previous section are that some people have to face extremely hurtful and complicated situations. Being pushed into forgiving can bring with it an intolerable burden, made worse if someone is told God wants everyone to forgive *now*, whatever the situation.

For Christians, a simple reading of the Bible often seems to make trying to forgive harder, and we need to explore more of what is meant by God's forgiveness and ours.

What would a "forgiving attitude" look like in practice? How does forgiveness relate to justice and truth-telling?

I will suggest that we should think of forgiveness as a process over time, and I'll look at possible stages we might go through as we try to put down our emotional and spiritual burdens.

Recent research into trauma has shed new light on the processes people go through as they try to recover and heal, and this new medical knowledge brings into focus some of the more complicated issues of healing from significant difficult events.

I'm going to use the terms "forgiving", "letting go" and "putting down our burdens" quite loosely, sometimes interchangeably, and at the end of this section I'll attempt to pull all the strands together and make some attempt to say what forgiving actually is.

CHAPTER 12

It's Not the Same for Everyone

*I hope that I am a man of a forgiving nature. Human
beings may be, can be, and indeed ought to be, able to
forgive on human terms, but ultimately it is for God to
forgive, and on his terms.*

(Gordon Wilson)

What I hope is clear from the stories is that sometimes the
things that happen to people are far from straightforward. For
example, when Louise was abandoned by Bob, and he refused
to pay a penny for the children, anything even remotely close to
forgiveness was going to be problematic.

Bob never apologized. He showed no remorse (despite
asking friends to forgive him), leaving Louise in a desperate
situation and completely abandoning his children. And whatever
could Louise's friends say to Bob? It was all very confusing.

What I'm getting at here is that human life and relationships
are complex, and some of the events that happen to us are so
deeply hurtful that our lives are changed for ever. And there is
always a different flavour to forgiving when the hurt is ongoing.

A stolen purse

If you bump into me and say "sorry" that's not a problem – of
course I will forgive you. But when someone stole my purse out

of my backpack on the London Underground, that had much more of a negative effect on me, and getting myself home again without my travel card, money or bank cards was terribly difficult. I had to ring my husband to cancel all my cards so no one could empty my bank account – and there were some personal items I lost which I found upsetting.

What would be the relevance of forgiving someone whom I don't know? I remember thinking that whoever stole it must need the money more than I did, but that wasn't much of a consolation in the confusions of the day.

But what if my home was burgled? What if someone came into my safe place where I live? What if they set fire to my house, damaging my photo albums beyond repair – all my photos of my babies that I can't replace? How would I ever feel safe in that house again? How would I deal with the sense of intrusion and violation?

That's much worse than a stolen purse.

Are some things unforgivable?

But what if some people attack me in the supermarket car park? They rape me, stab me, abduct my child and leave me for dead. They might rape or even torture my child. How can I forgive these heinous crimes – particularly while they actually hold my child captive?

As I researched this book I tried to listen carefully to people in a whole range of different groups, talking about what forgiving meant for them in their different situations. Below are some quotes I collected to show the complexities of forgiving for some people who have been through what Stephen Cherry, in his book

Healing Agony calls "shattering hurt" – overwhelming events that change someone's life for ever, often with them experiencing what doctors call post-traumatic stress disorder (PTSD).

> I was tortured for two years. They treated me as less than a human being. It is difficult to forgive someone who tortures you. There is no change. They go on torturing people. Can we forgive when there is no change?
>
> *A woman from Burundi*

> Justice is more important than forgiveness.
>
> *A woman from Bosnia whose whole family were killed*

> I'm not going to forgive them if they don't think that what they did to me was wrong.
>
> *A young man who was repeatedly raped by his father and uncle, who both said what they did was a good thing – teaching him about sex*

> Genocide is beyond forgiveness.
>
> *A man from Rwanda*

> To get behind the wheel of a car when you are drunk and wipe out four young lives just like that is unforgivable.
>
> *A woman whose daughter and three friends were killed by a drunk driver*

> How dare you? How dare you say that the man who murdered her should be forgiven?
>
> *A woman whose daughter was murdered*

Often I've heard Jewish people say "The Holocaust is unforgivable", and many share that view.

In these kinds of extreme situations, even to talk of forgiving is a huge struggle. Anything that we might call "fast forgiving" doesn't seem possible. Forgiveness in such circumstances would be a very long process of months or years. Like Julie Nicholson (whose daughter was killed in the 7/7 bombs in London), some would find it impossible in the early days. Some people would go as far as to say it is always inappropriate to forgive a murderer of a young innocent person.

Today on the news a man is in custody who murdered two policewomen. No one is talking about forgiving him. With the mood on the news, it almost feels morally wrong even to consider it.

Forgiving, in these kinds of extreme circumstances, is not as simple and straightforward as some Christian teaching seems to imply. It is no easier for the people in the stories in Section B. And yet some Christian pastoral care suggests that it should be.

"It's simple. You just do it!"

One man said to me:

> You just do it! Why do you make it sound so complicated?

He then went on to quote Gordon Wilson, whose daughter Marie was killed in the Enniskillen Remembrance Day bomb in Northern Ireland in 1987.

Like most people, I was deeply affected by the loving and generous words Gordon Wilson said after his daughter died. He was quoted in several of the many books I read, and in most it was pointed out by writers that this is how we should all forgive. Certainly I took his words to mean that he forgave the bombers and I remember being terribly impressed he was able to talk like that. And that became how I thought Christians should forgive.

Following Gordon Wilson?

There has grown up a belief in some Western Christians that this "instant" way of forgiving is how it should be done – as if "forgiveness" is some kind of blueprint you apply to all difficult situations and it solves everything, however traumatic. But this puts people under huge pressure, and what I'm exploring in this book is the potential damage that this belief in "instant forgiving" can do to those who have experienced a huge and traumatizing hurt.

When I read Anthony Bash's book *Just Forgiveness*, I was surprised to find that he didn't think that Gordon Wilson actually forgave the bombers, so I reread on the web what Gordon Wilson actually said. For example:

> I bear no ill will to anybody … not bitterness … I prayed for them last night.

Anthony Bash points out that at no point did Gordon Wilson say he forgave the bombers. I was astonished. But Bash is right: Gordon Wilson didn't say that he forgave (though I read later that he said he asked God to forgive them). So in Bash's terms, what he did was not "thick forgiveness".

I read Stephen Cherry's book, *Healing Agony*, and found he agrees. Gordon Wilson never actually said "I forgive them". In fact Wilson, in his book *Marie*, says: "I did not mention the word 'forgiveness', though many people believed that I had 'forgiven' the bombers."

So how did his words metaphorphose into words that got into dozens of books, radio programmes, and apparently into many people's heads as an example of quick and perfect Christian forgiving? Why is it that so many people, including the Queen in her Christmas Day broadcast in 1987, found his example so inspiring – "Mr Gordon Wilson … impressed the whole world by the depth of his forgiveness"?

What Gordon Wilson did do was refuse to get into the tit for tat revenge killings that were so much a feature of Northern Ireland at that time. He asked for no retaliation. He refused to hold on to any resentment. He had without any doubt a "forgiving attitude". As Archbishop Robin Eames put it, in the foreword to Gordon Wilson's book *Marie: A Story from Enniskillen*:

> His words, his attitude, his sheer human goodness and faith shone out like a beacon of hope in the darkness. Faced with the devastating loss of Marie his words of Christian understanding were to become an inspiration to thousands. What he said and did were of infinitely greater significance and meaning than the bomb and the bullet.

It is the importance of a *forgiving attitude* which is the really important thing, not the pressure for quick forgiving that is often seen to be how all Christians should forgive under all circumstances. For some of us it is a process that takes a long time.

Annoying reporters!

I've seen many examples on the television news of reporters holding a microphone up to someone's face who has just experienced a devastating event and asking, "Do you forgive them?"

What a terrible pressure to be under, knowing you are expected to forgive instantly. And what you might be able to say in those awful hours immediately following a tragic incident, when you are stunned, are not likely to be the words you might use a week or a year on. What if there is no justice? What if the person gets away with it? All of these future events are likely to alter initial words and emotions.

What we now know about experiencing some traumatic event is that the psychological impact can be so enormous in some circumstances that it can affect a person for the rest of their life, often seriously reducing the quality of their life.

Christians and forgiving

One of the purposes of this book is to address the huge problems caused for people who have been traumatized by the sort of Christian teaching that says forgiveness is easy, straightforward, and you must "just do it". So what does the Bible say about forgiveness? How do theologians interpret the words of Jesus?

It turns out to be much more complicated than I originally thought.

Key points

- Many Christians believe that we should all forgive straight away, whatever the kind of hurt and the impact of it.
- Some events can traumatize people, leaving them with long-term difficulties.

Further reflections

"His words, his attitude, his sheer human goodness and faith, shone out like a beacon of hope in the darkness."

(Archbishop Robin Eames about Gordon Wilson)

CHAPTER 13

The Bible and Forgiveness

To the Lord our God belong mercy and forgiveness ...
(Daniel chapter 9 verse 9)

"Instant forgiveness" seems to be part of much Christian culture, and some people in a caring role put hurt people under pressure to forgive. For example, John's pastor (chapter 6) told him he must forgive or God wouldn't forgive him. I think this is a simplistic reading of the Bible. However, a common theme in my conversations with people who have faced some hurtful event in their life is difficulty in saying the Lord's Prayer. They read the words: "Forgive us our sins, as we forgive those who sin against us" and they think it means that unless they forgive the person who wronged them, completely and instantly, they will be excluded from God's love.

I think this is so wrong, as I shall explain, but it is a very common misconception.

Another part of the New Testament which causes the same reaction is the parable of the unmerciful servant in Matthew's Gospel, chapter 18. So this chapter is mostly about that parable and about the Lord's Prayer.

Struggling to forgive

Let me make clear that I'm focusing here on people who

- are struggling to forgive
- say they don't seem to be able to forgive, or
- don't know how to forgive, or
- don't think it's appropriate to forgive, resulting in some confusion in their faith
- have tried to forgive but feel they have failed for a range of reasons
- want to put down the burdens of resentment.

These people are very different from others who are determined to take revenge and have set their minds against God. Wanting revenge is probably a normal human response after being subjected to a great wrong, but if it becomes a settled attitude, and if we continue to plan revenge, and live by the law of retaliation, that will add to our burden and we will not be behaving like one of God's children.

God loves you!

To get our bearings about the Bible, I want to start somewhere else.

When I was in California I went to some seminars led by a Christian theologian – I'll call him Sam. He spent the first hour talking about God's immense and unending love for all of us, quoting the Bible copiously. His main message was: "God loves you. He loves you unconditionally. There is nothing, nothing at all that can separate you from the love of God."

It was Paul who said in Romans chapter 8 verses 38 and 39:

> I am convinced that … [nothing] in all creation, will be able to separate us from the love of God in Christ Jesus our Lord.

Then, after coffee, Sam spoke for more than an hour about how if we don't forgive others, God won't forgive us. He gave some biblical examples, including the parable of the unmerciful servant that we are going to look at soon. He repeatedly said: "If you don't forgive *first*, God won't forgive you."

Two opposing beliefs

I was perplexed. It seemed to me that Sam was asking us to believe in two completely opposing views at the same time, so I asked him how we reconcile them. On the one hand we have God's unconditional love that will never end, and on the other we have God not forgiving us if we can't forgive others.

I was relieved that Sam looked a bit stunned when I asked him about those two opposing views. I hadn't been sure if it was me misunderstanding him. Sam said that he had never realized there were two opposing beliefs and he would go away and think about it.

The following week Sam told me he'd thought a great deal about what I'd said, but he still couldn't reconcile them. I found this a bit unnerving, but I was so grateful for his honesty.

You can't have it both ways

To me it seems clear. We cannot say that God loves us, and will never stop loving us, and also say that if we find it a terrible struggle to forgive instantly and completely, then we are "heading for hell", as one enthusiastic pastor said to me. I challenged that particular pastor on this, pointing out that I was sure God loved me, but he insisted I was doomed because of my struggles.

That has to be nonsense! It's a complete misunderstanding of the main message of Jesus of Nazareth, who demonstrated in his life and teaching God's love and compassion. Rather than living by rules, he condensed the Ten Commandments into two new commandments:

- Love God with all your heart, soul, mind and strength.
- Love your neighbour as yourself.

If Jesus really meant us to understand that any lack of forgiving on our part would result in us being "outside the love of God", he would have made it a bit clearer when he told his followers those two new commandments.

He might have added, "And by the way, if you don't forgive really quickly and completely, you will not enter the kingdom of heaven."

He didn't say that. And there was no eleventh commandment to Moses saying, "Thou shalt forgive otherwise thou art doomed!"

Sam (the theologian in California) was right to talk about God's unconditional love. But then he and others say that God's willingness to forgive me depends on me forgiving others. I think he was wrong about that. I want to say that God's forgiveness is there for all of us. God's willingness to forgive me isn't conditional on me forgiving others. God's forgiveness is there waiting. Of course, to receive God's forgiveness I must be willing to accept it, and that means not continuing to plan revenge, or continuing to live by the law of retaliation.

But I believe Sam was right to emphasize God's unconditional love. Here are some other thoughts from the Bible.

In the Old Testament God said to the people of Israel:

> It isn't because there are more of you that I love you, or because of anything you've done. I love you because I love you.
>
> (*paraphrase of Deuteronomy chapter 7 verses 7 and 8*)

In other words, God's love is not something to be earned. It is offered freely by a God who is loving, and faithful and just.

And, speaking of Jesus, John writes:

> In this is love, not that we loved God but that he loved us and sent his Son to be the atoning sacrifice for our sins.

And then:

> since God loved us so much, we also ought to love one another.
>
> (*1 John chapter 4 verses 10 and 11*)

God is a God who forgives.

Many of the books on forgiveness that I've read say that it is Jesus' parable of the prodigal son (in Luke's Gospel chapter 15 verses 11 to 32) that shows us most clearly how God forgives.

I particularly like the way Tom Wright, in his book *The Lord and His Prayer*, says that the story of the prodigal son could be called the story of the "Running Father". He explains that in Jesus' time, a man running would be as shocking in modern-day culture as if the "Prime Minister were to show up for the state opening of parliament wearing a bathing costume".

But the Running Father ran to his wayward, returning son to greet him with open arms, and it is this image of God's forgiveness that rings true to the rest of the Bible.

The God of the universe welcomes us with open arms when we "return home", because the main message of the Bible is of God's love towards us. We need to hold on to that when we come later to look at some of the hard bits of what Jesus said.

The background to Jesus' teaching: looking at the bigger picture

In order to understand the background to Jesus' words about forgiveness, we need to think a bit about what he knew his first hearers believed, and therefore how they would have interpreted his words. It's always important to look at the *context* of words in the Bible, in order to understand what Jesus actually meant.

As the New Testament scholar Tom Wright has made clear in many of his writings, the Jews of Jesus' time first understood "forgiveness" to mean "liberation":

- Sometimes the forgiveness word is linked to the exodus, when God's people were freed from slavery in Egypt.
- Sometimes it is linked to a later time when God's people

were taken to exile in Babylon, and from which they longed to be free.

- "Forgiveness of sins" was understood as something to do with being set free.
- Freedom was about the coming kingdom of God, when God would put his world right.

So "forgiveness" was not first about a person's individual relationship with God (though if course it includes that), but with the liberation of the whole community. That is why the word translated "sins" in the Hebrew Bible often describes "community debts" that are owed to God.

Jesus comes to announce the coming of that kingdom of God:

- Debts are cancelled.
- People are set free.
- Sins are forgiven.
- A new debt-free community comes into being, which reflects God's love, mercy, compassion and justice.

So Jesus' followers would have seen his words about forgiveness as including these bigger ideas. The coming of God's kingdom, which we pray for in the Lord's Prayer, is obviously a gargantuan idea. Our own personal experience of God's forgiveness, and the forgiveness which we can then show to other people, needs to be seen within this bigger picture.

I think that as we are invited to be members of God's renewed family and as we are freed and forgiven and loved, so we can learn to show something of God's kingdom in our lives.

That might be by

- showing our own loving and forgiving attitude
- the way we love and care for others
- our honesty and integrity
- the ways in which we seek out truth and justice.

The Lord's Prayer

In Matthew's Gospel, the Lord's Prayer comes in the Sermon on the Mount (Matthew chapters 5 to 7). It is first a prayer acknowledging our relationship with God as our loving heavenly Father (which actually would have reminded Jesus' hearers about the exodus, when God said: "Israel is my firstborn son" Exodus chapter 4 verse 22). Then it is a prayer about the coming of God's kingdom "on earth as it is in heaven". It goes on to talk about our need for God's blessing of sustenance (daily bread) and for deliverance from evil, and between them is the prayer for forgiveness.

When we read in the Lord's Prayer, "Forgive us our sins as we forgive those who sin against us", it cannot mean:

- "Forgive us because we have been forgiving", or
- "Forgive us in just the same way that we forgive", or even
- "Forgive us because in some way we have earned your forgiveness."

There is no sort of legal contract, as if God is saying, "If you do this, then I will do that." It is rather something to do with living the new life of God's kingdom. Where God's new life has been received, our forgiving others can be the natural sign of showing that God has forgiven us.

It simply reminds us first that God is a God who forgives, and then that the Christian community is to be a family of generous, merciful, loving and forgiving people. And we can be part of that family, and be that kind of person *and still have a problem struggling with forgiving after a hurtful event.*

I want to say a bit more about praying the Lord's Prayer in the next chapter.

We don't *earn* God's forgiveness

Tom Wright puts the case against the legalistic view some people have of forgiveness very simply. He says:

> Forgive us our trespasses, as we forgive those who trespass against us … *isn't* saying that we do this forgiving in order to *earn* God's forgiveness.

The italics are Wright's and it is this simple sentence that can release those of us who struggle to forgive from the sense that we aren't doing well enough. Many people I've talked to worry that God doesn't love them because they are struggling. We can't, and don't need to, earn God's forgiveness! *God's forgiveness is a gift, freely given for those that want it – a gift of love – part of what Christians call God's grace.*

Elsewhere in the New Testament it is very clear that it is as we allow ourselves to receive God's love and forgiveness that we ourselves learn to be forgiving people. Paul puts it like this in his words about the new life of the Christian community as God's people:

> … be kind to one another, tender-hearted, forgiving one another, as God in Christ has forgiven you.
>
> *(Ephesians chapter 4 verse 32)*

What do we do with Matthew 18?

When I have been talking to theologians, I have been intrigued to find that they were appalled that anyone would interpret the Lord's Prayer as a condemnation of those who struggle to forgive. As I said earlier, David Augsburger commented that this just abuses the hurt person all over again.

So, be reassured if you've been a victim of the "If you don't forgive, God won't forgive you!" threat. It is untrue. God loves you!

It's a bit harder with the parable of the unmerciful servant.

One pastor working with survivors of abuse who struggle to forgive said: "Whatever do we do with Matthew 18 – it throws up so many problems."

Jesus tells this story (in Matthew chapter 18 verses 21 to 35) of a servant who owes his master a vast amount of money – an over-the-top exaggerated amount showing it is a story to make a point rather than some accurate account of how to live our lives. The servant who owes the vast amount asks for mercy and the master cancels the huge debt. But then the servant refuses to release another person from a tiny debt. When the master hears of this he is angry with the unmerciful servant and throws him into the debtor's prison, reinstating the debt and expecting the servant to pay it all back.

Difficult words

Some people interpret this story to back up their belief that God will not forgive us unless we forgive others – apparently immediately and completely – and that is based on the difficult words in verse 35: "So my heavenly Father will also do to every one of you, if you do not forgive your brother or sister from your heart."

These words are difficult to understand in relation to the rest of the Bible, so I searched in many books written by eminent theologians and not a single one of them held the rigid view that Jesus meant that if we don't forgive, God won't forgive us!

I do not believe that the difficult verse 35 can possibly mean that God's forgiveness for us is entirely dependent on how well we forgive others.

God's overwhelming mercy

This parable is first about God's overwhelmingly generous compassion and mercy. It is a reply to Peter's question about the limits to forgiveness. Peter asks Jesus about how often he must forgive someone – seven times? Jesus replies: "Not seven times, but seventy times seven."

I'm pretty sure Jesus didn't mean that if a particularly irritating person hurts us 490 times, then when he does it again we lose our cool and attack the person! Of course not. Jesus turns Peter's question on its head. We are not to think about *how often* we must forgive. What Jesus means is:

- There is to be no limit to our mercy and generosity.
- It's about who we are as a person.

- It's about the state of our inner spirit – someone with no limits to their wish to share compassion.

Jesus wants us to be merciful to others, just as God is merciful to us, and one thing we can say about the unmerciful servant is that he didn't have the first clue about forgiving, mercy, or treating others in a way he wanted to be treated himself. He didn't have a forgiving and merciful attitude – which is what I think this parable is about. Matthew is conveying this parable of Jesus to his community to encourage them to live the life of God's kingdom in their relationships with each other. *But, as I have said, we can be a loving and merciful person and still be struggling with forgiveness about some specific incident.*

A softer view of forgiving

Anthony Bash points out that if we only read Matthew's Gospel (and read it in a particular way) we could come up with a very harsh understanding of forgiving.

If we read the Gospel of Luke, for example, we find a softer view of Jesus' teaching about forgiveness than we do in Matthew. In Luke chapter 15 Jesus tells the story of the lost sheep; the shepherd drops everything to find his one missing sheep, stopping at nothing till he finds it. The same is true of the woman who loses a coin. She turns the house upside down till she finds it. And then we get the story of the prodigal son.

This is a picture of God seeking us; whatever we have done, or not done, God focuses on us and goes on and on seeking until we are safe in the arms of the shepherd and taken home.

The harsher words in Matthew's story need to be set

alongside Luke's story of that determined shepherd, and the woman who is ecstatic when she finds her lost coin. It's further confirmation that the God who made the mountains and puffins searches for us, runs towards us, loves us – and will go to the ends of the earth to bring us back home.

The opposite interpretation!

The parable of the unmerciful servant is not primarily about our forgiving. It is mainly about God's overwhelming mercy and grace, which God's people need to reflect – *and this is the very opposite of the interpretation that it is about God condemning us for struggling to forgive*! We need to be very clear about this.

Struggling to forgive after some significant hurt is normal. Forgiving can be hugely difficult and we need time to go through the process.

So those who tell us that God won't forgive us unless we do our forgiving first are interpreting this parable wrongly – greatly adding to the burdens some victims already carry. It's about God's limitless grace and mercy. We can turn to God at any time and, even when we are struggling to forgive or let go, we can be confident that God hears us – and accepts us.

The Message

I very much like *The Message*, by Eugene Peterson. It is a translation (not a paraphrase) of the Bible into contemporary language. He ends Matthew chapter 18 by saying:

[The king said] "I forgave your entire debt when you begged me for mercy. Shouldn't you be compelled to be merciful to your fellow servant who asked for mercy?" The King was furious and put the screws to the man until he paid back his entire debt. And that's exactly what my Father in heaven is going to do to each one of you who doesn't forgive unconditionally anyone who asks for mercy.

(The words of Jesus in Matthew chapter 18 verses 34 and 35)

Here we have a translation that fits exactly with the rest of the Bible. Matthew's parable is about *responding to the cry for mercy*, which God does, and which the unmerciful servant in the story did not do. Matthew wants the Christian community he is writing for to learn – and we need to learn – to be merciful and forgiving people, and when someone asks us sincerely to forgive them, we must not harden our hearts against them.

So, as Stephen Cherry points out:

A simplistic reading of the challenge to be forgiving in Matthew 18 and the Lord's Prayer can lead us into some very dangerous waters.

What do these difficult parts of the Bible have to say to us?

- God calls us to be part of his kingdom, live as disciples of Jesus, and show something of his love, mercy and justice in our relationships.

- We need to treat other people with respect, mercy and love – in other words, treating people in the way we would like others to treat us. (I think this is part of what Jesus teaches us in the Sermon on the Mount.)

- We need to be forgiving and loving people, and as God extends to us huge mercy and forgiveness, so we need to bask in that enormous love and enable that love to flow through us to those around us.

- We need to hold on to the picture of God in the story of the Running Father, who ran towards his wayward son, arms open in love and forgiveness.
- We need to read all the Gospels to get a full picture of what Jesus was teaching us about being merciful and forgiving people.

Key points

- God says: "I love you because I love you."
- It is wrong to insist that our forgiving is a pre-condition of being loved and forgiven by God.
- God loves us and nothing can separate us from that love.
- The Lord's Prayer doesn't mean we must try to earn God's forgiveness.
- The parable of the unmerciful servant is mostly about God's generosity. It's the story of the prodigal son that teaches us more about forgiveness.
- God's mercy and forgiveness is a free gift of grace.
- God expects us to be merciful to others in response to the mercy we have already received.
- It's God who forgives! It's God who gives us the power to be loving, merciful and forgiving people.

Further reflection

"Father, I have sinned … I am no longer worthy to be called your son." But the father said … "Quickly, bring out a robe … a ring … sandals … let us eat and celebrate; for this son of mine was … lost and is found!"

(Luke chapter 15 verses 21–24)

CHAPTER 14

God's Forgiveness and Ours

God in Christ has forgiven you.

(Paul in Ephesians chapter 4 verse 32)

Being told things such as "If you don't forgive, God won't forgive you!" can cause people to turn away from Christianity. This picture of a "tit for tat" God – "I'll only forgive you if you forgive first" – just isn't there in the Bible, and it's not the God I know because it paints a picture of a God withdrawing love from someone already desperately hurt.

I've seen so many people trying somehow to work themselves up and try harder and harder to forgive some great wrong, when all that happens is that they get into such a state that healing is somehow sidelined; this seems to have been happening to John, the person I referred to in chapter 6.

Struggling to forgive doesn't "undo" our status with God. We are children of God because we believe in Jesus – and it is this belief, this trusting in the enormous love and grace of God that marks out a Christian, not whether we've managed to forgive someone who hurt us deeply.

Here is another statement I have heard many times, which also causes confusion:

"Jesus commanded us from the cross to forgive."

I actually think it is devastatingly wrong! What Jesus said on the cross was: "*Father,* forgive them; they don't know what they are doing."

This holds a great truth about forgiving – all forgiveness comes from God! It is this fact that I have seen change some people from their terror that God doesn't love them (because they struggle with forgiving), into people who can smile and allow themselves to bask in God's love. For example, when I said, "But it's God who forgives!" to Teresa, her eyes lit up. She smiled, and later she said how much it helped her to be released from the obligation she felt that she must forgive now.

"It is as I allow myself to see the huge extent of God's forgiveness of me that I learn how to forgive others," said my friend Penny, and I think she's absolutely right.

It may be that some of the people who find it harder to forgive haven't allowed themselves to let God love and forgive them – *really* love them. Do we really just let God's love and forgiveness pull the burden from us? I think that is what we can try to do – imagine ourselves walking along with no backpack; nothing to weigh us down.

Perhaps it is that amazing lightness and total freedom that we need to immerse ourselves in. Maybe this is one strategy to try in order to ease our process of putting down our burdens. It's something I try to do when I say the Lord's Prayer.

Can I still pray the Lord's Prayer?

When we are not feeling very forgiving, Brother John of Taizé makes a very important point:

> When we feel we are not yet able to forgive, can we can still pray the Lord's Prayer? Yes, because ... we must not forget that the Our Father is not an individualistic prayer but the prayer of the community of the church.

We are praying alongside the millions of others who in some sense are carrying part of our burden for us. The whole church is sustaining us and the forgiving we are still struggling with is merged into the forgiving that millions of others are able to do. We're not alone.

When we are praying

We must make a distinction between our confused thoughts as we struggle to forgive and recover from trauma, and our words and thoughts to God *when we are actually praying.*

If we are actually saying to God in prayer, "I'm going to take revenge", then we're heading in the wrong direction. It isn't for any of us, ever, to pretend that we can predict what God thinks about the spiritual state of anyone, but I think it might be possible, if someone persists in turning away from God's love, and is determined to kill, or in some way try to destroy someone, then they might themselves be turning their back on God.

> "Revenge! Revenge! Revenge!"
>> *Ken, played by Michael Palin in the film* **A Fish Called Wanda***.*

Revenge?

We can turn away from vengeful thoughts gradually over time as we ask God to help us lay down our burdens of resentment. (This could take years, but that's OK.) But if we persist in praying "I'm going to take revenge", or asking God to strike down the person with a long slow lingering death (I remember thinking this when someone hurt me and my family, turning our lives upside down), then we are in trouble. These are normal human feelings, but they are working in opposition to God's mercy and grace. As we pray it would be better to ask God:

- To take the whole burden of our resentments and our inability to forgive away from us: "Please take all this hurt from me. I'm dumping it all on you because I know you can take it."

- To plant inside us the *possibility* that we *might some day* think of laying down all that resentment. "Please make me willing that one day I might possibly…"

It really does only need to be that initial "one day I might… if you will give me the strength…"

Revenge destroys our soul

The First Wives Club is one of my favourite films, but when the three women are planning revenge on their husbands, they end up fighting and raging at each other. It's once they start making their centre for helping vulnerable people that they start to feel happier and get back the love they have for each other. The end product is a great crisis centre – the result of turning from revenge and focusing on healing.

Similarly, in the brilliant BBC production of *King Lear*, Michael Horden changes dramatically as he begins to talk about revenge. He starts off angry, but once revenge is on the agenda, he metamorphoses into a madman. Revenge destroys our soul.

Forgiving and loving people

God's way of leading our lives is not for us to say to those who hurt us, "You owe so you must pay." That isn't the way towards God's kingdom. We are to allow God to love us, forgive us, and it is this that enables us to learn to be loving and forgiving people.

But this doesn't suddenly make our loving and forgiving attitude easy. It doesn't take away the struggle. It doesn't mean we can't strive for justice, as we will see in later in the book. And we might find we have to do what Louise did in chapter 9, when her husband abandoned his family and had no contact with them. Louise felt forgiving was inappropriate, "leaving the forgiving to God".

Our mental images

If you have been struggling with forgiving, or feeling that it's impossible to forgive, take comfort from the Running Father and the prodigal son. God runs towards us – and it is those open arms of God that can be our image when we struggle with saying the Lord's Prayer, or when we encounter those with rigid views. It can give us patience to keep going "every day… oh… every day".

Another mental image I use at times when enthusiastic people tell me I "must forgive, or else…" is God as a mother hen. (This is an image from Luke chapter 13 verse 34.) I shelter in complete safety under her wing. There I have no burden. I just allow myself to be loved and accepted.

Forgiveness and healing

I wish Richard, Marion and John (chapters 3 and 6) could have been released from their burdens and know they are protected and loved. I'm sure this could have sped up their healing. So many people have said to me, during discussions about forgiving:

> The healing comes first. The forgiving can only start when people feel they are well on the road to healing.

I think that Teresa (page 115) was moving towards some healing/liberation when she realized that all forgiveness comes from God. And I would add to this that survivors of abuse, and possibly those who've experienced other trauma, need to *feel safe – at least safe enough* even to begin the forgiving process. I'll go into the effects of trauma in chapter 21, but it's important to raise this issue of safety here. Forgiving can start when we feel safe enough, and probably not before.

I was working with a group of clergy talking about responding well to survivors of abuse. I told them of my many experiences of survivors of abuse being told that if they don't forgive, God won't forgive them.

"I would never say that to someone so hurt," said one clergyman. He then went on to say what he preaches about forgiving: "If we don't forgive, God won't forgive us." I didn't have the courage to point out to him that he'd just said what he said he wouldn't say!

A problem when we are teaching

Most people I know who teach agree with me that we can stand up and say some things only to find that at the end, someone says, "I'm glad you said xyz" but often I'm sure I haven't said xyz! I've said "abc", nothing like what they think they've heard me say.

This seems to be one of the odd things about life. We can think we've said "abc" but that's not necessarily what people hear. So if we add into the problem the fact that most deeply hurt people will be in at least some anxiety, maybe easily distracted and so on, they could "sieve" out some of the detail – or even the main meaning of what someone is saying.

In this kind of situation:

- If we unthinkingly and without explanation say: "If you don't forgive, God won't forgive you!" a stressed person is going to hear: "God rejects me."
- Going through trauma can often lead to depression, and the negative thinking that goes along with depression is going to focus the hurt person onto the worst case scenario: "I'm heading for hell."

This kind of thinking pulls traumatized people away from the very source of their healing – the support of caring friends and the loving arms of God.

Where our heart is

Going back once more to the story of the unmerciful servant, Jesus speaks of forgiving "from your heart". It's clear that "where our heart is" becomes important. We need to have a heart that is close to God – listening to our Maker. If we keep close, then divine love and mercy will be flowing through us to others around us. We will want to put others before ourselves. We will want to care for others, including those who have hurt us. (Eventually! We are unlikely to be able to think this way until we have healed considerably from the trauma.)

I need again to make the vital point that we can have a heart close to God and still be struggling with some big event from which we are healing – sometimes desperately slowly.

And we can have a heart close to God, and let go of a wrong thing someone did to us and still decide that we want to keep away from the person because we don't like or trust them. Letting go of something doesn't mean that there has to be a restoring of the relationship. We might be able to go back to being friends. Or we might not. And that's OK.

Relax and let God ...

We can relax in the knowledge that just handing all our struggles and burdens to God is the best thing to do in those early stages – even if what happened was years ago.

So we don't need to fear saying the Lord's Prayer. We need to remember:

- Forgiving is a process. It is rarely a one-off event – though for some people the initial moment of wanting, or intending to forgive can be a specific time we will remember for ever.

- Mostly forgiving is something we do every day. It is about our attitude to life and towards those around us.

- We can say the prayer with the image of God's protecting wing over us, knowing that nothing can ever separate us from that love.

Key points

- All forgiving comes from God.
- Meditating on the love and forgiveness we have already received from God can help us to be more generous to others.
- To hold onto resentments and to live by the law of "you owe so you must pay" is not the way of God's kingdom.

Further reflections

"Love was his meaning"

(Julian of Norwich)

"… though I walk through the valley of death, I will fear no evil, for you are with me … goodness and love will follow me all the days of my life, and I will dwell in the house of the Lord for ever."

(Psalm 23 verses 4 to 6, NIV 1984)

CHAPTER 15

It's All a Matter of Attitude

Many people think that Jesus is the most forgiving man that ever lived. I think you'll find that many people will say that even if they aren't Christians, but hold to some kind of moral code.

(Nancy)

Nancy said this to me some time ago. We talked for a while about her beliefs (she was quite strongly against any kind of religion) and I began to ask other acquaintances who wouldn't call themselves Christians where they got their ideas about forgiveness.

- "You have to forgive, don't you? Otherwise you get all screwed up inside," said Elizabeth.
- "People who don't move on can be so negative to be with," said Jane.
- "Life is too short not to forgive," said Robin.

As a teenager, when I was trying to work out what Christianity was all about, I found forgiving very confusing. I got the impression that Jesus wants us to be "doormats" – "just walk all over me", turn the other cheek when someone hits you, and that kind of thing.

Gentle Jesus, meek and mild

As a child in a violent home, I had learned not to hit back because that just made everything worse. As I read the Gospels, I found it confusing to know how Jesus actually wanted us to behave.

Most people seemed to take "turn the other cheek" as not retaliating, and that made sense, but all this meekness and allowing others just to go on being mean left me feeling that it was wrong to stand up for justice. I just got bashed if I stood up for my mother, but I still wanted to stand between her and my stepfather. Did Jesus really mean that she just had to go on taking her beatings day after day? I felt this lacked reality – but no way could I say that at church youth clubs!

A doormat?

Most of the Christian teaching at the church youth clubs supported what I'll call the "doormat syndrome" – we just had to take whatever was done to us without question.

And it is this kind of teaching that I think has led to considerable misunderstandings about what it means to be a Christian, and our ideas of justice and forgiveness. If we think back to Diana's story of domestic abuse in chapter 5, we see Christians allowing violence to go on – expecting a mother just to turn the other cheek when she is attacked.

Does Jesus want us to be hit again?

It was with considerable relief that I came across the theology of Walter Wink in his book *Engaging the Powers*, quoted by the Linn family in their book, *Don't Forgive Too Soon*.

What Walter Wink says is that we've got completely the wrong impression about what Jesus means in the Sermon on the Mount when he says, "if anyone strikes you on the right cheek, turn the other also".

Jesus doesn't at all mean us to be hit again!

Why does Jesus specify the *right* cheek? According to Wink this is because if we were a servant in Palestine, our master couldn't use his left hand to hit us because that hand was only ever used for unclean tasks. So he must hit us with his right hand – with a backhanded swipe – because this was the way to show someone that they are beneath you.

So turning the other cheek (our left cheek), our master can still only use his right hand – but he can no longer backhand us. If he hits us again he will have to use an open hand or fist. But this was something *only done between equals* – so turning the other cheek would be us "[reclaiming our] dignity and communicating that [we] refuse to be humiliated", as the Linn family put it. In other words, it would require my oppressor to treat me as an equal.

The second mile

Jesus goes on to say, "if anyone forces you to go one mile, go also the second mile". The Linns comment that in Palestine at that time, the Roman occupying soldiers could require the locals to carry their packs, but only for one mile (more would be illegal forced labour). So to "go an extra mile" would put the Roman soldier in a difficulty. You have regained your dignity, you have chosen your own response and you have refused to behave as a victim.

So all this "letting people walk all over us" stuff isn't actually what Jesus meant. He seems to have meant much more about justice and not allowing ourselves to be put down by those who have power over us. It's much more about humans being equal in the sight of God, and us valuing others and being merciful and honest, and being peacemakers who "hunger and thirst for righteousness" rather than warmongers who retaliate and want to win, whatever the argument. They value their own dignity before God by non-violent resistance to oppression.

The Beatitudes

When Jesus was giving the Sermon on the Mount he talked about the meek people being blessed. I can now see this isn't about us being doormats. It's about non-violence, valuing other humans and loving our neighbour, and when Jesus tells us to love our enemies, I think that also is about us needing to recognize that we are all children of God, whatever we have done or not done.

For me, this means learning not to think of those who have hurt me as utterly bad people. We all make mistakes, and learning to put ourselves in the other person's shoes is a vital aspect of us growing up and thinking in a reflective and mature way.

If I had been born where he was ...

One of the most startling bits of television I ever saw was Archbishop Desmond Tutu talking to people who had been hurt in The Troubles in Northern Ireland. A woman said she realized that if she'd been born where the IRA man who killed her son had been born, she might have thought like he did – and done what he did. How extraordinary that was! I could hardly believe what I heard. She was acknowledging that she could have been just like her son's killer if she'd been born the other side of town.

This is what I believe is important for everyone to think – not so much: "Oh, poor dear, look what an awful home he comes from, no wonder he's a murderer." This sounds too much of an excuse, though it contains some truth. What I mean is that when someone has hurt us deeply, we need an acknowledgment that everyone does things wrong. We all hurt people at some point in our lives.

Of course, some people's actions seem to be so awful that we might think of them as utterly evil. And it's impossible to imagine what their motives might be. But it's important not to judge people; a very difficult thing to do! It's not for us to label someone as "evil" – however right that feels in some instances.

Our attitude to life

My interpretation of what I think Jesus asks us to do in his various teachings is to have an attitude to life that is loving, merciful and forgiving. We could call this a "Beatitude Attitude" and it would involve:

- listening to the other person
- not always being sure it is us who is right
- learning to see things from the other person's point of view
- learning to value others and seeing them as someone that God loves – in other words, not demonizing the person

who hurt us, but instead praying for them. And it's OK to pray that God will give them what they deserve!

It's about being the kind of person:

- who doesn't instantly snap back at someone when they disagree
- who is pleasant to be with, and
- who will always give the benefit of the doubt – checking what has been done and said first before roaring in with our rage of disapproval, throwing anger around in an alarming way. (You can tell I've met some people like this!)

It is this loving and forgiving attitude that I think is what we pray for in the Lord's Prayer.

A spirit at peace

We are asking for our inner spirit to be at peace and in touch with God's Spirit, and for us to treat those around us – God's children – with respect. This is particularly true in situations where we are with those less powerful than we are – people who work for us, for example.

Some of the powerful people in the stories in Section B (vicars, counsellors etc.) abused that power, putting people down and failing to have a loving and forgiving attitude to the hurt people around them.

Changing attitudes

As we try to dump our burdens, trusting in the love and forgiveness from God to enable us to have a forgiving attitude, almost certainly we will find our attitudes to those who hurt us change – gradually over the years. We begin to understand what it might mean to love our enemies and pray for those who hurt us.

But I think this is a very advanced stage to reach. I still find it quite hard to pray in anything remotely like a loving way for the couple who attacked me! I'm not thinking ill of them. I just feel a bit vacant about it. But I pray that God will bless them and help them out of their strange ways.

Loving those around us

There are several places in the New Testament where Paul urges Christians to be loving and forgiving towards each other. For example, in the letter to the Ephesians, Paul says:

> Put away from you all bitterness and wrath … and be kind to one another, tender-hearted, forgiving one another, as God in Christ has forgiven you.
>
> *(From Ephesians chapter 4 verses 31 and 32)*

This could look like more evidence that we "must forgive or God won't forgive us", but it's always important to look at the context of things in the Bible. As various writers point out, Paul is writing to Christian people in a church, and it almost certainly isn't a group of people up against torture, incest, rape, murder, burglary, mugging and other devastating crimes. It's probably more in the context of people arguing and getting cross with each other – in other words, the stuff of daily life for most of us.

Paul is telling the Christians to have a forgiving and loving attitude. I conclude from this that however hurt we have been, however much the hatred has become part of the culture in which we live, and however outrageous the atrocity, we do need to dump as much of the bitterness and twistedness as we can.

Key points

- Jesus's teaching about being meek and merciful doesn't mean we have to let people walk all over us.
- We should stand up for justice where we need to do that.
- Jesus teaches us to love those who hurt us, and this can mean not demonizing people.
- "Loving our neighbour" includes having a generous and forgiving attitude.

Further reflections

"In this is love, not that we loved God, but that God loved us …"

(1 John chapter 4 verse 10)

CHAPTER 16

Letting Go

The fact that I don't bear them any malice might be partly a protection on my own part. It would be extremely stressful for me if I were to spend a lot of time thinking of recrimination or about ways of trying to "get back" at these people.

(Gordon Wilson, referring to the bombers who killed his daughter Marie at Enniskillen)

After the IRA bombed London in 1992 when the Revd Dick Lucas's church was badly damaged, a journalist asked him if he forgave the bombers. Dick Lucas replied that he wasn't aware that anyone had asked for forgiveness. What an incredibly brave and honest answer that was, and it emphasizes one of the really big issues about forgiving – what do we think about forgiveness when there has been no apology?

Some theologians (in chapter 2, I referred to Anthony Bash's "quintet") suggest we should use a different word instead of "forgiving" when we are talking about putting down our burden when we haven't had an apology. In other words, if we let go but haven't had an apology, some say that isn't actually true or "thick" forgiveness.

On the other hand, for many people it is OK to use the word "forgiveness" even when all five aspects of Bash's "quintet" aren't present. For example, on Christmas Eve 2012, Alan Greaves was brutally murdered on his way to his local church to play the organ. His widow, Maureen, has publicly said that she has forgiven the men who killed Alan. I doubt she had an apology. She said, "I realized that if I was able to forgive, other people would be able to forgive as well... If I was full of hatred, other people would pick that up and be affected by it. I had to be forgiving."

Maureen admitted that she found forgiving the killers one of the hardest things she'd ever done. It did not mean that she didn't want justice for Alan. She did not have any warm feelings towards the killers "but I do know that God loves them, and I try to keep that in mind". She also said that forgiving the killers gave her a huge sense of relief. She could put her energy into helping the family to cope "rather than being eaten up with anger and hatred" (from an article by Joanna Moorhead, *The Tablet*, 21/28 December 2013).

Even though there was no apology, and Maureen did not "forgive" in the strict sense of "thick" forgiveness, her letting go of anger and hatred is what most of us would recognize as a forgiving attitude. Perhaps we can think of letting go as part of the meaning of forgiving.

What is crucial for those hurt through no fault of their own is that they find their way back to mental health, contentment, and are able to live a fulfilling and loving life. What matters, under the big umbrella term of "forgivenesses", is that we are going on our journey through life without the awfulness of burdens that significantly negatively influence our lives.

New Testament words

At this point it is worth noticing that the Greek word which is translated "forgive" in the New Testament (*aphiemi*) is also used in some places to mean "let go". (It is also used for "put away", "send away", "cancel or pardon a debt"). And the noun translated "forgiveness" (*aphesis*) is used to speak of "deliverance", "freedom", and "remission" (or even "sending away") of debts. So it comes in Luke's Gospel when Jesus is speaking of his mission: "*release* to the captives ... and let the oppressed *go free*" (Luke chapter 4 verse 18). St Mark talks about the "baptism of repentance for the *remission* of sins" (Mark chapter 1 verse 4). There is also the story of the time when Jesus' disciples explained to bystanders why they were untying a colt to take to Jesus, and the bystanders "*let them go*" (Mark chapter 11 verse 6). Or, to give one more example from Jesus' words, "if anyone wants to sue you and take your coat, you must *let go* your cloak as well" (Matthew chapter 5 verse 40).

An umbrella term

I think the New Testament allows us to understand "forgiveness" as an umbrella term, perhaps reflecting different aspects of the forgiving process? (This is discussed in chapter 25.)

When we see the word "forgiveness" in the New Testament, we need to understand that it's something to do with liberty and the coming of God's kingdom. The forgiving actions towards others can sometimes be described as "sending away debts" or "letting go".

So God's forgiveness in a sense "lets go" of the debts to him which our wrongdoings have created; they do not simply accumulate against us. So maybe letting go is a good term for us to use, especially for people who have been hurt and where there is no apology.

Forgiveness can heal

The language of letting go can be particularly helpful to hurting people, because to speak of "forgiving" feels too overwhelming – especially when we think that what was done was "unforgivable", or that at the moment we just can't forgive. In my experience, letting go can be a more acceptable term for those for whom the word "forgive" has such negative connotations, perhaps because they have been threatened or pressurized in some way ("You must forgive!"), resulting in a sense of horror over the whole idea of forgiveness. And when we remember how closely words about forgiveness are related to words about salvation and health, we can think of the process of forgiving as letting go of some of the hurts and burdens and painful memories we are carrying because of wrong done to us, and of discovering something of God's freedom and healing.

The poet who wrote Psalm 103 brings these thoughts together:

> Bless the Lord, O my soul, and do not forget all his benefits
> – who forgives all your iniquity, who heals all your diseases,
> who redeems your life from the Pit, who crowns you with
> steadfast love and mercy...

Letting go and our mental health

One way of thinking of letting go, particularly after what Stephen Cherry calls an "outrageous atrocity", is to see it in terms of "letting go for our own mental health".

- We want to be free.
- We want to be released of resentments and feelings of revenge.
- We don't want to get "bitter and twisted".
- We long for healing of painful memories.
- We can let go of the feeling that we have to get even.

And of course, letting go for our own sake does not in the least mean that we should not still seek justice.

To think of letting go can help us to get further into the whole messy process of healing. We can start the process of:

- moving beyond our denial
- acknowledging our anger
- bargaining our way through our grief until we can reach a point of accepting that we have this heavy load weighing us down, and we could dump it all – eventually.

Is it selfish?

I was talking with a group of people, including some clergy, about the idea of letting go for our own mental health, and how helpful that has been when I've been working with young people.

"Oh, that's very selfish," said one clergyman.

I can't get my head around that. Having spent years of my life going in and out of mental hospitals, being depressed for decades and talking to a bewildering number of psychiatrists (and finding that not much of that actually helped!), I take my mental health very seriously.

Working with survivors of abuse and with people who are depressed, it seems to me that one of the most important aspects of human well-being is to put as much effort as we can into caring for our mental health.

There is absolutely nothing even remotely selfish about that! Letting go for my mental health makes me a happier and healthier person, and I'm able to have positive and loving relationships with those around me. Believe me, that's a zillion times better than being a drugged zombie slumped in an armchair in a mental hospital.

Dismissing the past

I've found another strange view that some Christians hold. They can give the impression that *if we forgive, that wipes out the past* – as if the awful event hadn't happened, and should not be thought about or spoken about again. This can be very hurtful. It can cause a great deal of pain – and it is an inaccurate message to give out.

If someone mows you down in a car accident when they are drunk, breaking your spine so you will never walk again, no way does forgiving wipe out the past. It can be similar with other wrongs people have suffered. Letting go is likely to change your attitude and lead you into a more contented life – but you will always be unable to walk. Forgiving doesn't change the past. But it can change our inner attitude as we move towards healing.

How much choice do I have?

One of the central issues around what we actually do when we forgive is how much of the process of letting go *is about our will*. On the web, Jill Saward, the victim in the 1986 Ealing vicarage rape case, thinks it's *all about our will*. She was quoted as saying: "It's not whether you can or you can't forgive; it's whether you will or won't" (headline in *The Telegraph*, 8 March 2006).

This feels much too harsh to me, loading more lead bricks of guilt into the backpacks of those who have been overwhelmed by some event. It puts far too much emphasis on me needing to grit my teeth and work myself up to the point where by some supreme effort I will manage to forgive. But this is where John was when I met him on the healing course we both attended (chapter 6). He put so much effort into trying to forgive that he seemed not to be progressing with his healing.

There is some truth, of course, in Jill Saward's point; there must be some role for our will in forgiving. On the other hand, Jim McManus says it isn't merely our will:

> Forgiveness cannot be commanded as a mere act of the will. Who could command the heart to heal, the soul to enlarge, by issuing an order? Could I become twice as good a golfer or twice as slender by commanding it?

Again, it feels as if there is some truth here in that there is a long process to go through (for most people) to forgive, but how McManus puts it doesn't feel quite right either. My will must be involved, even if it is simply wanting to feel better and realizing that might happen if I decide (an act of my will) to try to stop thinking about the hurt and working at not allowing myself to ruminate.

But I think what Jim McManus might mean is that *desperately wanting* to forgive, working on my rumination, and so on, still wouldn't be enough.

I think the process of forgiving is:

- less to do with my will, and
- more to do with me allowing God to love me, and
- me intending to live the best life I possibly can.

It's coming back to us needing to be people with a forgiving and loving attitude (but we might still have a big problem with someone), and I think that comes from listening to those around us, and to God – by which I mean being someone who, with God's help:

- is loving
- is in the process of developing a merciful and forgiving attitude
- hungers and thirsts after justice, and
- allows God's love to dominate their life.

It's bigger than just my will

When I first became a Christian as a teenager people talked about "sanctification", by which they meant a process through which we grow closer to God once we have faith. People seem not to use that word now, but "discipleship" probably means something similar. I take this to mean living a life of caring for others just as Jesus and his disciples did. So faith is not just something I know about in my inner being – my soul – but something that is about loving. It's God's loving arms around all of us, shepherding us along our journey – filling us with love for our neighbour, and doing things to make the lives of those around us better.

Yes, there must be quite a bit of our will involved in that process, but it's much bigger than an act of my will.

Those who go in for insisting forgiving is easy and quick are trivializing that beautiful process of being loved and shepherded along, with our burdens lightened as we determinedly dump things (using our will) and our loads are lovingly removed from our backs as we grow closer to God.

Discovering forgiveness

Looking back on my own processes of letting go, it has always felt as if I was trying to find forgiveness; indeed, that was the original title of this book. In the end I think I discovered forgiveness, sometimes quite unexpectedly. I see this as a result of being loved and nurtured both by God and by those around me.

But I think I also had to be looking for and working at that forgiving.

Key points

- Some instances of forgiving might not always be "thick" forgiving.
- Forgiveness is an umbrella term with several meanings.
- We can let go for our mental health.
- Forgiving is bigger than my will.

Further reflections

"People who are dying need to let go of their past hates and difficulties if they are to have a peaceful death. Often it's forgiving themselves for things they have done, or family problems. Letting go is so important at the end of their life."

(Ginny Dunn, palliative care nurse)

CHAPTER 17

Justice for Everyone

... what does the Lord require of you but to do justice, and to love kindness, and to walk humbly with your God?

(The prophet Micah, Micah 6 verse 8)

Many Christians think that both forgiveness and justice are vital concepts when some wrong has been done. However, while I was researching this book, and my previous book about recovering from childhood abuse, it became clear that survivors of abuse found themselves pushed and shoved into forgiving with no apparent attempt to acknowledge that justice is also important.

- "Why can't I have justice?" one woman asked.

- "If you are going to forgive someone, I think you have to hear them say sorry – and mean it. She won't say sorry. She just says she never did anything. How can I forgive that?" said a young man who had been sexually abused by his aunt from a very early age.

- "People at church keep telling me to forgive and forget, but he's just getting away with it. He could do it to someone else if we just let him go free," a young girl said after disclosing that her father had sexually abused her for years.

A diagram of forgiveness and justice

It seems that to take a balanced view of forgiving, we need to involve justice. I visualize that on a "forgiving and justice line" like this:

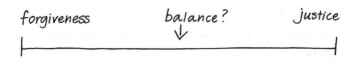

As I talked to people about forgiving, sometimes sharing some of the stories I'd collected for this book, it became clear that many people felt that all Christians should be at the left hand end of the line, focusing on forgiving. However, other Christians who had faced extreme difficulties said that they thought that seeking justice was very important. For example, Fraser said: 'God in the Bible is a God of justice, and I'm up at the right-hand end of your line.'

Fraser was typical of people in the early stages of recovery from a traumatic event.

Many who held the view that we "must forgive or God won't forgive us" believed that we should always be at the left-hand end – at the extreme end.

A balanced view

The God of the Bible is both forgiving and just – both aspects are important, and it seems to me that it is one aspect of living

143

a happy and contented life that we find some sense of balance between the two.

Many people who have been desperately hurt will never get justice of any kind:

- The murderer got off on a technicality.
- The rapist got a "good" lawyer.
- The hit and run victim is just left in limbo.
- The judge said it was just one person's word against another so the case was dismissed.
- The person who hurt us is dead, and we never dared say anything when they were alive.
- The drunk driver who killed gets a short jail sentence and families are left angry.

"We didn't get justice for our Janice," one father said on the news.

> Forgiveness before justice is "cheap grace" and cannot contribute to authentic healing … Once justice has been accomplished, even in a limited way, forgiveness becomes a viable opportunity. Prior to justice, forgiveness is an empty exercise.
>
> *(Marie M. Fortune)*

When no justice is possible

When we know we have no way of getting justice it could be the time to move ourselves along from seeking justice to letting go of our hurt. Our seeking justice needs to be balanced with practicality; there's very little point in striving for something that we can't ever get.

But some people – for example, Nazi hunters – seem to give up their own family life and comfort to pursue evil. I always find that heart-wrenching, but their striving against injustice and evil is amazing. I sometimes ask myself whether they should just give up.

Aspects of living

The "forgiving and justice line" on page 143 is only one way of seeing that tension between two important parts of life. We can add other dimensions to the line – I like the cross that includes both love and mercy because it is those four aspects of Christian living that are so important when we are discussing forgiving:

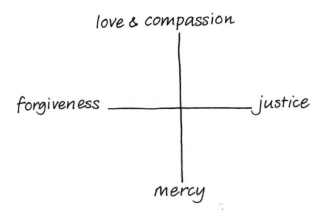

Perhaps when we balance all these aspects of Christian living we can live lives full of the fruits of the Spirit – love, joy, and peace – and be aware of the resurrection power of the Holy Spirit.

Forgiving is important

Sometimes people have assumed that I'm saying that forgiving isn't important. I'm not saying that at all! Of course forgiving is important – very important – but *it is just one aspect of our Christian life.* Over the years of researching this book, I've felt with some of the "you must forgive now or else" people, they were looking at life in a rather odd way, *as if forgiving was the most important* part of life.

It's important. But so is having mercy and compassion, loving God and our neighbour, feeding the hungry, having a loving and forgiving attitude to those around us, and practical things such as using our money to help those less well off than we are. The list is enormous, and whenever I hear yet another traumatized person tell me that they had been told by their pastor that God won't forgive them, I want to protest that forgiveness needs the balance of justice, love, mercy, and compassion as well.

A tension between forgiveness and justice?

In the story of Jamie, when he was hit by Stan, the vicar and many people insisted that the way for the community to heal was for Jamie's family to forgive Stan. But from the family perspective, laws had been broken (child abuse and assault) and because Stan insisted on saying he didn't do it, and because he clearly had a drink problem, they thought it best to take him to court to get justice for Jamie and to push Stan into realizing that he had a problem, and needed to get help.

On the "forgiving and justice line", the vicar and most of the congregation were at the very end of the line next to "forgiving"

– they seemed to have very little sense of what justice for Jamie might be. Jamie and his family wanted justice, and were much further towards the right-hand end of the line – they were more balanced.

However, it was clear that Jamie's family wasn't at the far right end. They knew there would be a time to forgive – indeed, they were "in the process of forgiving", as Jamie's grandmother told me, but felt that it was still right to pursue justice. It's possible to forgive someone but still take them to court, because justice and obeying the laws of the land are fundamental to societies living at peace. Forgiving isn't the same as a legal pardon. A crime of assault had been committed. We can't just ignore crimes, because we risk lawlessness breaking out.

Forgive and forget

Some people I talked to were saying that "forgive and forget" was the way forward. Brush it all under the carpet. Forgive and forget. Move on.

I think this is unbalanced. I don't think it's right for forgiveness to take precedence over justice. It's just convenient. It's much easier for someone to say

- "just forgive" than it is to come alongside the hurt person and say
- "I'll be here beside you, helping you to work through it so that you find some kind of peace in your soul."

To be with someone in their pain takes time and effort. It isn't clear-cut and dealt with instantly – as "forgive and forget" might be. But it's impossible to forget traumatic things! And as Dr

Lewis Smedes said in his personal communication, "We have to remember in order to forgive with any meaning"!

Wishing our abuser well

In conversations about forgiveness, people sometimes disagree with me by pointing out that Jesus told us to love our enemies and to pray for those who hurt us. Yes, I agree that is an important aspect of our healing once we are beyond the initial stages of the hurt. It's pretty difficult to do when we're still trembling and having nightmares! But even then it does not remove the need for justice.

> I think when we get to the stage of wishing our abuser well, we can say that we have truly forgiven them. I found I started to want the best for them, but of course, that might mean a prison sentence so that they will sort their life out and work out the impact they've had on their victim.
>
> *(Linda)*

Loving our neighbour, including our enemies, may mean that we reach a stage where we "want the best for them", as my friend Linda put it. We want justice not just for ourselves but for them too. A prison sentence might be the best, or coming face to face with their victim so that they realize the hurt they inflicted.

Forgiving doesn't, and mustn't, mean we ignore justice.

Good resentment

I've seen situations where there is a total lack of justice for someone deeply hurt, and I came to see that it's OK to have a "good resentment". Although we mostly think of resentment as something we want to get rid of – because bitter resentment can be very destructive – some writers point out that when we stand up for some injustice, that could be because we have a "good" kind of resentment. For example, I saw the musician Alice Cooper on television saying how angry he gets because there are children in America who go to bed hungry. There are thousands of hungry and poor children in Britain as well, and I think that is appalling. The "goodness" of a nation, I think, is judged by the way it treats its most vulnerable members, and at the moment there are countries that seem more interested in some people getting richer than they care about the degrading poverty of others.

That for me is something to feel resentful about – in the same way that presumably those who abolished slavery were moved to anger by that appalling trade. I think it is through channelling our anger, and "good resentment", that we can change the appalling things about the society we live in.

Key points

- Forgiving needs to be balanced with justice, mercy, and love.
- Some hurt people will never get justice.
- We can forgive but still want justice.
- Engaging with the messiness of our lives and our struggles to forgive is much harder than simply saying to someone "just forgive". This is easy to say, but damaging to the person's healing.
- Balancing love, forgiveness, mercy, and justice can be a way to live a life of peace and joy.
- As we go through our healing journey we could aim to get to the stage where we want the best for those who hurt us.
- As we work for justice, we can have "good resentment".

Further reflections

- Understanding the effects of trauma on people is crucial if we are to treat them with love and compassion.

"It is certain, in any case, that ignorance, allied with power, is the most ferocious enemy justice can have."

(James A. Baldwin)

"True peace is not merely the absence of tension: it is the presence of justice."

(Martin Luther King, Jr)

CHAPTER 18

Trivializing Forgiveness

Cheap grace is the preaching of forgiveness without requiring repentance … Communion without confession, absolution without personal confession. Cheap grace is grace without discipleship, grace without the cross, grace without Jesus Christ…

(Dietrich Bonhoeffer)

To lift a phrase from Dietrich Bonhoeffer's book *The Cost of Discipleship*, to trivialize forgiveness and make out that it is "easy" is "cheap grace".

What is happening when we forgive when:

- there is no apology
- there is no sincere act of repentance for causing such hurt
- we are failing to give out the message that wrongdoing is wrong
- we can still be stunned and unable to touch our feelings after an event?

If we just forgive perpetrators of crimes, we could be leaving them able to go on hurting people. This could have been the case in Jamie's story (chapter 4) when Stan hit him, and when I was unexpectedly attacked (chapter 8).

We can't just ignore crimes. It allows injustice to win, and a society without justice is going to get very messy.

People I've talked to seem to be trivializing forgiving when:

- they used the words "just forgive" with the clear indication that it was easy to let go of the whole incident
- forgiving is completely the wrong thing to be trying to do, as in Lizzie's story with the sex offender (chapter 10)
- someone is struggling with all kinds of overwhelming feelings and the letting go is going to be a long and costly journey. Instead of coming alongside the victim and supporting them, they are judged as a bad forgiver. "Just forgive. It's easy. You just do it," as one vicar said to me. What this does is make the victim out to be the one who is in the wrong because they are struggling with forgiving. And it can prejudice people against the word "forgive". That's not helpful!

The process of forgiveness calls upon all our faculties.

(John Monbourquette)

Although forgiveness has a range of meanings, it only ever applies when some moral wrong has been done to one or more person when it is the wronged person who can forgive.

Forgiving, or letting go, is a crucial part of healing, but it cheapens forgiving – trivializes it – to try to force people into a superficial act of instant forgiving when:

- they don't really understand what it is that they have to forgive
- the healing journey isn't far enough along

- they are still raw and grieving
- they have developed mental health issues such as depression or post-traumatic stress disorder.

To treat forgiving as a kind of cure-all for everything is a huge mistake, causing hurt people devastating pain on top of the awfulness of the initial event.

Sometimes forgiving isn't appropriate

There are some circumstances in which forgiving can be inappropriate.

- It may be wrong to forgive someone, or give them the impression that they are forgiven, if they do not accept they have done wrong, and simply want the freedom to go on repeating their crime. This is "cheap grace" – using forgiveness in a completely wrong way, demeaning the forgiveness of sins. This is what was happening in Diana's story of domestic abuse when she was told to forgive her husband (chapter 5).

- Many people believe that God forgives us only when we say, and mean, sorry, and that therefore we humans can only really forgive when someone admits their wrong and says sorry. In Jamie's story of being hit by Stan, his grandmother repeatedly said to me that they felt that the child abuse was morally wrong, but would have forgiven Stan quickly if he'd admitted hitting Jamie and said sorry.

- It is inappropriate for counsellors or anyone else to push someone into forgiving, especially if they haven't had an apology, as in Richard and Marion's story. As I've said, many theologians make the point that without an apology, there can be no true forgiveness – or "thick" forgiveness as Anthony Bash calls it.

- Equally, it is wrong to push a hurt person into forgiving because that could be moving them too fast through the healing process, meaning that their recovery can be jeopardized, and could result in the damaged person being hurt all over again, making their situation even worse. This was true for Marion, Richard and John (chapters 3 and 6). Diana came to think that she had done damage to her children by insisting they forgive their father (chapter 5).

So forgiving is a much more complex idea than some people think. It's certainly not something we must force ourselves to do when we are in the early stages of healing from a traumatic event. But having said that, we may well know that we want to forgive – and are intending to forgive or let go when we can.

It isn't easy!

Although it probably is true that "forgiving is good for you", as Archbishop Desmond Tutu has said, what I'm saying is that forgiving can be hard work. It can be gruelling, leaving us exhausted and discouraged. It isn't easy when the difficult event caused us to have overwhelming feelings of loss and anger, and when our lives are so bad that normal living is impossible.

For a Christian, wanting to be a loving, merciful and forgiving person, having what I've called a Beatitude Attitude, facing the results of trauma is hugely difficult.

- How can I keep my inner spirit focused onto being loving and caring?
- How can I stay a forgiving and merciful person when I'm struggling to forgive some devastating act?
- Why is it that although I desperately want to forgive, somehow I just feel confused, frightened – and guilty because I feel I should be able to forgive, and I don't *feel* even remotely forgiving?

For many people who have endured trauma, there can be numerous mental health issues to deal with: dissociating, anxiety, depression, and so on. These cause dis-ease and this profoundly influences our spiritual life, and therefore any attempt at forgiving.

Key points

- Fast forgiving can be problematic.
- It's important not to push people too early into forgiving when their healing journey is only just starting.

Further reflections

"Forgiveness is not the misguided act of condoning irresponsible, hurtful behaviour. Nor is it a superficial turning of the other cheek that leaves us feeling victimized and martyred. Rather it is the finishing of old business that allows us to experience the present, free of contamination from the past."

(Dr Joan Borysenko)

CHAPTER 19

Truth Telling and the Link to Justice

Truth is followed by justice.

> *(David Cameron, British prime minister,*
> *after the publication of the Hillsborough disaster report)*

For some people who have been through a difficult event, the truth about what actually happened is unclear.

- Sometimes victims don't know exactly what happened.
- Sometimes childhood memories are very deeply buried.
- Sometimes other people try to prevent the truth being known; for example, rape victims are told "it's just your word against his" so there is no case to go to court.

How can we talk about forgiving in these circumstances?

I read several books by psychologists when researching this book and often I found the belief that "Once we know the truth the grieving process can begin", and "You cannot lay the past to rest until the truth has been told".

Striving for truth

As I write this in 2012, twenty-three years after the Hillsborough disaster, when ninety-six people died in the crowds at a football match in 1989, a report has been published that finally gets to the truth. It wasn't drunken and disorderly fans that caused the deaths. It was the fault of the police.

I watched the debate in the House of Commons on television and over and over again bereaved families were praised for their tenacity in campaigning for the truth. Newspapers and other media told lies, blaming the fans, and it was revealed that the police changed 164 statements about the day. This criminal tampering with evidence "perverted the cause of justice", deeply insulting bereaved families.

Truth followed by justice

Now that the truth has come out, hopefully some kind of justice will happen. Those who held all the power at the time – the media and the police – will have to account for their abuse and criminal actions.

There were many apologies from the government this week, and most significant of those were from the people in government at the time of the event, when efforts to get at the truth years ago were squashed, creating a "false narrative" that was spread around, concealing the truth.

It's these "false narratives" that those who have been deeply hurt know about, leaving perpetrators free to abuse again and again. This is particularly true for abused children, when they don't know what to say, or who to say anything to. Added to that are the threats: "Don't tell or I will kill your dog"; "No one will believe you."

And a terrible fear sets in, engulfing the child's life. Tragically, for some people, this state of fear can go on for a very long time. (And telling the person that Christians shouldn't fear isn't helpful!)

Feeling safe enough

Being afraid is a common symptom after a difficult event. Sometimes when I say this to people who haven't experienced something that has devastated their life, they are surprised that fear is so debilitating and prevalent. "Why would someone be afraid after being raped?" one man asked me. I found it hard to respond to that because I think it's obvious why!

Fear is a dominant emotion in meetings for survivors of abuse, and needing to feel safe is hugely influential in my life. There are some things, such as going into a crowded place, which I can only do with considerable emotional cost (extreme anxiety and nightmares etc. in the days following).

Love casts out fear

I know in theory that Christians are supposed to believe that God's love has taken away all their fear, but actually working that out in daily life can be tough. It's too easy in some circumstances for me to start telling myself "you shouldn't be afraid". But my body trembles. I feel sick. If I go too far down the road of "shoulds" and "oughts" I just end up feeling guilty, which doesn't help at all because then I think what a hopeless and useless person I am!

But, as Judith Herman (a psychiatrist who specializes in trauma, see chapter 22) says, we can only face the truth of an event – really engage with what actually happened – if we feel safe enough. She says that establishing safety is the first thing to do for us to get into the stages of recovery. Without that sense of safety, we are unlikely to have the emotional strength to say "this happened and it was devastatingly painful".

When truth is obscured, that process of needing to face the truth is delayed because we don't know what the truth is.

> The first step towards healing is to find a place where you feel safe. This might be a physical place – or somewhere in your head – or both.
>
> *Liz Mullinar, founder of Mayumarri Heal for Life Centre, near*
> *Sydney, Australia*

Part of the meaning of love in a pastoral situation is to provide that safe space in which a hurting person can discover that they are loved – ultimately by God. It is the love of God that casts out fear. Many of us need a lot of loving to overcome our fears.

Colluding with the perpetrator

If we see people being hurt or downtrodden, I think it's important for Christians to stand up for justice, not collude in the wrongdoing. This colluding can be several different things:

- Telling the victim they must forgive. This puts the guilt and pressure on the victim rather than the perpetrator.

- Trying to suppress the truth. I was told not to go to the police after I was attacked because it would "bring disrespect to the church". How weird is that? How could it possibly reflect on the church? What did this say about the attitude to truth and justice of the people saying that?

159

- Any kind of suppressing the truth builds up the silence and secrecy that almost always surrounds abuse of any kind. It's secrecy that is so pernicious and destructive when abuse is happening.

As I'll discuss in chapter 22, often all that perpetrators ask us to do is to be silent and to do nothing. This just feeds on the fact that most of us find it easier not to engage with those who have experienced huge hurts. It's that odd kind of denial that if we don't really listen to what happened, we won't act, and maybe the whole thing will just go away – especially if we put all the burden back on the victim with threats of God rejecting them if they don't forgive *now*. This is colluding with the perpetrators and it obscures the truth.

Time for Action

Some churches in Britain (Churches Together in Britain and Ireland) worked together to produce a book called *Time for Action*, telling the truth about the effects of sexual abuse, include abuse by clergy. Some years later *Promoting a Safe Church* was published by the Church of England and the Methodist Church, which included advice about supporting survivors of abuse, and this was followed by the Church of England report *Responding Well* – a guide to helping Christians understand and respond appropriately to the devastating "disintegration of self" that can occur following abuse, particularly childhood abuse.

The church, like other big organizations, often hasn't been good at addressing issues of abuse, especially clergy abuse.

The truth hasn't been allowed to come out, leaving the victims in a state of disintegration, angry and so debilitated that they sometimes can't work, or have normal human relationships, particularly intimate ones.

What was needed was truth telling. Then some justice.

> Few if any issues in recent years have so stained and compromised the credibility of various Church institutions and hierarchies as the record of ignorance and evasion over questions to do with the abuse of children and adults by Christian professionals, especially clergy. Honesty about this is painful, but essential for the Church's health and the Church's mission. [The *Time for Action*] report is sometimes devastating reading, but it is timely, necessary and – if we are prepared to hear and act on some unwelcome truths – ultimately hopeful.
>
> *Rowan Williams, Archbishop of Canterbury, on the back cover of*
> ***Time for Action***

The truth will set you free

What *Time for Action* did was tell the truth. Without truth we know we are not heard. Without truth we can feel trapped – overwhelmingly burdened. It's truth that can release us. Sometimes we need enough of the love that casts out fears to enable us to feel safe to face the truth which sets free.

> Now we know the truth we can move on.
>
> *(A father after the trial of his daughter's murderer)*

But sometimes big organizations, such as the church, police, the health service and so on, can tend to "close ranks" when some awful event happens. How can the truth come out then?

Some notable police shooting incidents in which someone is killed without any clear reason have been followed by an enquiry by police – investigating themselves! It's hardly surprising the report just buries the truth – no one is found to be at fault – leaving families devastated. There is no explanation of why their loved one was killed.

Standing up for justice

This is the kind of abuse of power that seems so common in big organizations and with those in power colluding with perpetrators, leading to frustration, anger and crushing any search for justice and truth telling. Silence and secrecy prevail.

It was so good to hear this week the bereaved relatives from Hillsborough being praised by Members of Parliament for being determined to get to the truth of why the football fans died. And I was delighted to see Doreen Lawrence, the mother of murdered teenager Stephen Lawrence, walking with the Olympic flag at the opening ceremony of London 2012, sharing the task with others who have made it their life's work to bring about justice and peace. Doreen Lawrence kept up her pressure to have the murder of her son properly investigated by the police. She went on and on striving for the truth to be told and for justice for Stephen.

Forgiving?

In difficult circumstances, forgiving seems to require superhuman emotional and spiritual strength – not things that are in plentiful supply if there is post-traumatic stress disorder involved.

And there is always the issue of the abusive person being left to repeat their acts. One of my friends who was sexually abused by her vicar went to the bishop to tell him what happened. But it was just my friend's word against the word of the vicar, so nothing was done and the man was left working in a church where he had easy access to children and young people.

Sometimes in this situation, at least until recently, clergy have just been moved to work in another church. It's obvious that those who have been sexually abused by a priest are sometimes:

- left powerless
- frustrated
- fearful of another person being abused as they were
- confused about their spirituality
- angry at the apparent lack of responsibility taken by a big organization where it seems to be easy to bury the truth.

No one is responsible. "Close ranks. We are more powerful than the victims so if we all just keep quiet, it will all go away."

Except that it doesn't. It's left burdening people who were innocent, dragging them down into depression and the kind of self-loathing that comes with the guilt following abuse. Yes, it's odd. The victim was innocent. Someone more powerful than them abused them. But it is the victim who is left with overwhelming guilt.

Then they are told "just forgive".

An unreserved apology after truth is told

Following some truth telling, in February 2012, Bishop Paul Butler wrote a letter of apology on behalf of the Church of

England, expressing the "great sorrow and deep regret" for the lack of action and sensitivity by the church in response to those who disclosed abuse. He writes:

> The Reports prepared last year by Baroness Elizabeth Butler-Sloss and before her, by Roger Meekings are particularly damning of the past safeguarding procedures going back to the 1960s in the Church of England and for that I can only say we are deeply sorry. On behalf of the Church I would like to take the opportunity provided by the publication of these reports to express our own unreserved apology for those cases where we failed to take the action that we should have taken to prevent harm being caused to children and vulnerable adults. It is a matter of great sorrow and deep regret for the Church and we recognize the profound and damaging impact on all those who have been affected. We are grateful for the personal commitment of many of those who have been affected, to ensuring that the church faces up to these difficulties. This has helped us to become a safer place and to learn more about how to respond well to victims who have had the courage to come forward.
>
> *(Bishop Paul Butler, General Synod Report of Proceedings July 2013)*

One survivor friend said how helpful it was to know the church is at last taking the issues seriously.

Campaigning to uncover the truth

Those who strive for truth and justice (or to use Jesus' phrase: "hunger and thirst after righteousness") can sometimes be seen as a nuisance. "Why don't they just shut up?" can be the attitude.

Of course, sometimes it feels as if campaigners are only loud complaining moaners! I've sometimes found individuals so negative that it is hard to be in the same room as them. But that doesn't make what they are doing wrong. The loudness of some who seek truth can be because of those in power seeming to be deaf and blind to the truth, and at times apparently deliberately lying and "protecting their own".

Who can blame victims of huge wrongs for being more frustrated than forgiving in situations like that? For some people I think that even letting go can still leave them with personal pain and confusion.

The inability to cope and have enough emotional strength isn't a sign that they haven't forgiven! I've been talking about this with my friend Wendy who has long-term chronic fatigue syndrome. She's been told many times by Christians that she's ill because she hasn't forgiven. But *she knows* she has forgiven her abusers.

We can forgive and still be vulnerable with physical illness and mental health issues because being involved in a traumatic situation often has long-term consequences – particularly when the truth has been obscured and there has been no justice.

Reconciliation?

One important point about truth telling is that even in the best of circumstances, where the truth comes out and maybe there is even an apology, there is no inevitability about reconciliation. To be reconciled seems to me to mean that there is some *restoration of the relationship* that was there in the past, or a new one made. Some people are pleased to be part of restorative justice programmes, and these seem to be healing in some circumstances – particularly where truth is told.

But reconciliation? It will depend on the circumstances, but I can understand some people in South Africa feeling pretty annoyed that when the truth was told, abusers sometimes got away with extreme violence, even murder. If someone I loved was killed and the attacker was free, I don't think I'd think much of the idea of "reconciliation". However, the truth and reconciliation work in both South Africa and Northern Ireland has been healing for many. For others it could seem more like colluding with wrongdoers – but if there was genuine remorse, a renewed relationship might be possible.

Speaking out for victims

Campaigners are often speaking out for victims, demanding truth telling, and that can be so healing for people who have been hurt. But others are just silent and let the wrongdoing carry on.

> First they came for the communists, and I did not speak out because I was not a communist.
> Then they came for the trade unionists, and I did not speak out because I was not a trade unionist.
> Then they came for the Jews, and I did not speak out because I was not a Jew.
> Then they came for me, and there was no one left to speak out for me.
>
> *(Martin Niemöller, talking about the inactivity of German intellectuals following Nazi rise to power)*

Key points

- Truth telling is vital for good mental health for individuals, communities, and organizations.
- Finding the truth is a crucial aspect of healing from wrongs.
- Truth precedes grieving, healing, and justice.
- Truth must be told before there can be justice.
- Truth telling prevents the silence and secrecy that enables wrongdoers to go on repeating their crimes.
- Still having emotional or physical difficulties following a difficult situation is common and not necessarily a sign that the person hasn't forgiven.

Further reflections

- Even after truth is told, justice still isn't possible for many victims.

"It is not only much more conducive to an authentic relationship to report our true feelings, but it is equally essential to our integrity and health."

(John Powell)

CHAPTER 20

Saying Sorry: Apologies and Burdens

We failed big time. We can do nothing other than confess our sin, repent, and commit ourselves to being different in the years ahead.

(Bishop Paul Butler, Chair of the Church's National Safeguarding Committee, speech to Church of England General Synod, July 2013)

Bishop Paul, apologizing on behalf of the Church of England, raises an important issue: can someone apologize for something they didn't do? Does their apology have any meaning? Or can they only regret that something awful happened, and acknowledge what was wrong?

To apologize about something and really mean it must involve at least some sense of repentance – turning from the wrong and being determined never to repeat it – or, in Bishop Paul's case, working towards changing the institution of the Church of England so that it acts differently. Without that, they are just shallow and meaningless words. We've probably all seen it: "I'm sorry!" said without a jot of sincerity.

However, in one sense, I don't think you can repent for someone else. Repentance is primarily a personal thing that we need to feel very deeply within our inner selves. It is us facing ourselves and recognizing that what we did or said was completely unacceptable, and being determined to address the wrong and change direction. I think institutions can be said to "repent" if an apology is linked to an acknowledgment of wrong and a determination to act differently.

When Tony Blair, the British prime minister, said sorry to the Irish about the total lack of British action to help during potato famines of the eighteenth and nineteenth century, hopefully that contributed towards the recent easing of the relationship between the British and the Irish – easing "The Troubles": the bombs, the killings, the raging hatred on both sides for centuries.

Perhaps Tony Blair's apology for the then British government of the nineteenth century, just leaving a million people to die of starvation, smoothed the way for Queen Elizabeth to visit Ireland during her Jubilee tour in 2012, something that seemed impossible a few years ago?

So I think this kind of apology, from someone who wasn't personally at fault, nonetheless has huge power to help healing. We will feel comforted by someone – anyone – coming alongside us and feeling what we are feeling, saying they regret what happened and acknowledging that it was wrong. They are "sorry" that we had to go through it. But it can be more than this.

Institutional abuse

Sometimes there is "institutional abuse", such as the finding in England of "institutional racism" amongst the police following the Stephen Lawrence murder. While one member of an institution can't apologize for what another member did in any personal sense, nonetheless, as in Bishop Paul's case, one member of an institution can stand up and shout – apologize for the institution – and insist on changes in practice, and justice for victims.

If there is evidence of some sort of institutional abuse, particularly if it is followed by some kind of cover up by others, an apology is needed from more than the perpetrator of the wrong. An apology by leaders of the institution is appropriate. And they can do more than regret. They can also call the institution to repentance and to a change in the system.

Yet more baggage

But there is an added complication. I see survivors of abuse who feel they were wronged by someone working for "social services", or "the church", or the "national health service", becoming more and more weighed down as they go on demanding an apology from these large institutions.

Of course it is appropriate to want an apology. Survivors of abuse deserve an apology just as Jewish people do about the Holocaust. But I don't think an apology can be *demanded*.

If we go on demanding apologies from people, or institutions, or big organizations where there is no clear institutional abuse and where the perpetrator cannot be identified, all we are doing is adding to our load of resentments that we are carrying around with us.

We get dragged further and further down into the pit of resentment and rumination, where we will sit in that devastating confusion that results when we demand an "impossible" apology. If we are in that kind of "impossible situation", it's us who have to *change our attitude* in order to get out of the pit.

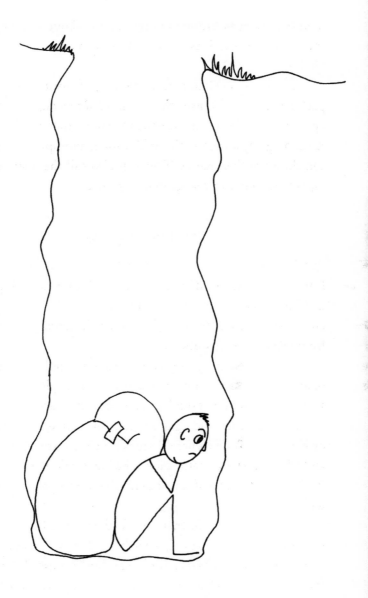

The effects of forgiving on the perpetrator

Many writers suggest that our forgiving can affect the person who hurt us. Clearly that would be true if we were in contact with the perpetrator and we said, and meant, "I forgive you." I think the person who wronged us might feel better if they actually wanted to be forgiven. I have a sneaking feeling that the couple who attacked me might think I was crazy if I knocked on their door and said, "I forgive you." I think they thought that what they did was a good thing!

But I wonder, when we forgive someone (with or without an apology), God sees the hurtful person in a different way? I don't think it's possible to know this, and it certainly isn't one more reason to justify pushing a victim into forgiving. But when Louise (chapter 9) left the forgiving of her husband to God, I think in some way she was asking God to forgive him. Maybe that made a difference to the way God saw her husband?

When we do something wrong and then apologize, it is such a relief to know that the person we hurt has forgiven us. So of course, being forgiven has an effect on the perpetrator. But the situation is much more complex and tangled when the person who wronged us hasn't or won't apologize, or can't because they are dead.

Be the first to say sorry

An interesting point about who can say sorry is made by some writers who point out that problems are rarely one-sided – all situations are, they say, at least to some extent the fault of both parties in situations that go wrong. So these writers say it's best for us to make the first move – be the first to apologize – perhaps making it easier then for the other person to say sorry.

Yes, this makes sense, but where these writers are wrong is that it is never a child's fault in abusive situations – never. *It's not the fault of both parties*. It's always the adult who is in the wrong. However short the girl's skirt is, however naughty a child is, any kind of child abuse is wrong, with absolutely no blame on the part of the child – because the child has no power.

The principle is the same in an abusive situation where there is a big power difference between those involved; for example, a doctor and patient, a priest and parishioner, a teacher and pupil, and the boss and a worker.

Key points

- It's not always clear that we can apologize for something we didn't do.
- But "regret" or saying sorry can be comforting and can heal relationships and communities.
- Trying to get an apology from a group that is never going to say sorry can just load us down with more baggage.
- Saying sorry first can sometimes be right, and can ease the forgiving process.

Further reflections

"Life may not be the party we hoped for… but while we are here we might as well dance!"

(Nikki)

173

CHAPTER 21

Why Can't We Shrug it Off?

I don't understand why survivors of abuse can't just shrug it all off. For some of them, the abuse happened years ago. Why are they still worried about it?

(Joseph)

In my discussions with clergy and others who said they hadn't had a hugely difficult life event to face, one question keeps being raised – why can't people just forgive and then they will be OK?

I was teaching at a conference for pastors about safeguarding children in the church (it's known that paedophiles tend to join churches in order to have access to young people), and Joseph asked me about why survivors of abuse can't just "shrug it off".

I told him about the damage it can do to people if they hold down their emotions that are boiling up in their inner world. It would be like holding the lid onto a boiling saucepan – something will explode. Emotions we try to hold down will come out some way unless we listen to them and try to deal with them. Held down they are likely to burst out unpredictably and sometimes catastrophically when there is some trigger that reminds us of the trauma in our past.

I thought I was OK

Janet spoke up and said she'd learned this the hard way. She told us that she was a counsellor at a major traumatic incident in Britain and she believed she was OK afterwards. She thought she'd resolved it and worked through her emotions from seeing all those dead people and hearing the screams of the injured.

Then she was watching the television news one day about another major incident, and she completely fell apart. She said that all her memories came flooding back from the first incident and she didn't know what was happening to her. She'd been a social worker for years and saw herself as a "together" person.

"But I broke down," Janet said. "It's very dangerous for our inner well-being to shrug it off. It can take ages to recover from trauma."

I turned to Joseph. "Thank you," he said, and smiled. "I've never been through any 'difficult event' as you call it, so I had no idea about all of this."

Working through the issues

Moving from our boiling saucepan to the image of our heavy backpack, I think that "shrugging it off" can add unexpected weight to our burden. We might think we're doing fine, but in the long term, that unexpected weight is likely to wear us down. And the unpredictable explosive catastrophe is a possibility.

Signs we have unresolved baggage in our backpack are:

- When we go "over the top" because of some small incident it's a sign there are unexplored things lurking in our soul. For example, anger over something trivial, or Janet breaking down.

- When we are depressed, that can mean our inner world is not at peace.

- When we are constantly ruminating on something that happened a long time ago, there is probably something there that we haven't thought through regarding the implications for our mental health.

- Anxiety or panic attacks that seem unrelated to what is going on are bound to be about something unresolved in our inner world.

Getting a balance

It can be hard to know when we've done enough inner exploring of our backpack to be sure we've thrown out of it those potentially explosive hurts and memories. But some people find writing in a journal helps, or talking to a friend or therapist.

Most of us have probably at some time thought an acquaintance was making too much of something but, of course, it's never our place to say "get over it".

Each of us is responsible, and in control of, our own backpack, although this may not be totally true if we are having mental health problems at the moment. But it must become true as we heal from our mental dis-ease. But what one person may recover from in a year, another person may take a decade or even a lifetime. (More about this in chapter 23 about limbic lag.)

Different responses

People make different responses to "difficult events". There is likely to be a different response because of the enormity of some things – murder, rape, or torture are much more overwhelming than the theft of a purse.

But it's important to note that a flasher in the park may make one little child giggle and shrug it off (or that's the way it looks), whereas another little child may have nightmares for a month, cling to his mother and refuse to go to school, and he may become anorexic by the time he is twelve.

The factors in the after-effects of significant hurts seem to be:

- the sense that the person made of the hurt in their inner world at the time it happened, and

- how they process that over the next few days and weeks, and

- the care they receive in recovery from the event, and

- the impact of the incident on their mental growth and development over the months and years.

Adults respond differently, partly because of their childhood. If they had a secure childhood and felt loved and valued, they may heal from traumatic events much more quickly than someone who struggled in childhood. Psychologists talk about our "attachment" (drawing on the theories of John Bowlby) and what this means is that a child who feels loved is likely to make a secure attachment to their mother, or primary caregiver, and probably also with the rest of the family.

However, those who have had a chaotic and/or abusive childhood, and didn't make a "secure attachment" with their primary caregiver when they were very young are much more likely to be strongly affected by something such as abuse. With good parenting, a child who is raped stands a good chance of managing his life better than a child who is left to cope on her own. I think it was because of my early childhood experiences of abuse that I reacted so strongly to the attack I experienced as an adult. It brought too many ghosts to the surface, causing my life to degenerate into chaos.

How do I start to heal?

My own experiences, and walking beside my friends who are survivors of abuse, has taught me that we are unlikely to recover from trauma without at some point facing it full on, with help, and recognizing that what happened was devastating. This can take ages because we need to feel safe enough to acknowledge the depth of our hurt – the opposite of "shrugging it off".

On holiday recently I fell badly during a run onto black gravel, skidding along onto my right hand so that lots of the gravel was embedded underneath folds of skin. I stood by the washbasin, willing the bits of gravel to come out, telling myself, "I'll be fine. It will heal anyway."

But I came to see that I was wrong and went to a doctor. It was excruciatingly painful for me to let him rub deeply into my wounds to get out all the grit, but looking at my hand now, a few weeks on, it has healed beautifully.

I had to face reality – I had to go through the pain to achieve that healing. In a similar way we heal from difficult events by facing the level of our hurt (gradually and with help) and admitting our depth of pain, and acknowledging the mess it has made of our life. It's only then that we learn to put down the load.

Putting down the load

Many times in my life I've been told I'm too introspective. Of course, we don't want to be too introspective. We need to get a balance. We need to remain outward-looking and care for others, but also develop enough self-awareness of our inner world through meditation (I think of this as listening to God rather than saying words), or writing in our journal, or talking to a friend and so on, in order to sort out our inner world and lay down our burdens.

Working on "Inner Child" issues

When I was working with a therapist, Ruth, as my memories of sexual abuse many years earlier were crashing into my life, I stumbled upon the book *Recovery of Your Inner Child* by Lucia Capacchione.

Working with my Inner Child was the most healing thing I did as I struggled with my symptoms of post-traumatic stress, and the principles of accessing our Inner Child are very simple.

Find a quiet place where you feel safe enough and where you can write and draw. Start with your pencil in your usual writing hand and ask your Inner Child a question, such as, "How are your feeling right now, little Suzie?"

Then put your pencil in your non-dominant hand and write or draw a response. It will be all over the place! Stick with it. Give yourself time, especially the first few times you try this.

Eventually I found that little Suzie was frightened and feeling horribly abandoned and rejected. I hadn't realized any of that and as I worked through those feelings I became aware that I had deep issues of whom I could trust. Could I trust Ruth? Could I trust David? Could I bear to acknowledge what I really felt? Could I cope with looking at my nightmares and flashbacks, instead of just shutting them out of my mind in order to survive?

Once I worked through those uncovered emotions, I was able to work through the anger and terror. Looking back on all that awfulness now, I can see that any attempt to "shrug it off" would have been disastrous, but working through it all has helped me to dump some of my burdens, be able to come closer to forgiving, and become less anxious and able to feel contented and at peace.

Lightening the load

I don't think it's right to tell someone to:

- "move on"
- "get over it"
- "forget about it", insinuating they need to "get a grip", and they're "being pathetic" because they can't just "shrug it off".

What can help us to dump stuff is:

- encouragement to keep working at it and to keep healthy by eating well and taking exercise (this can help to stop depression setting in)
- counselling or therapy
- chatting to a friend
- doing some kind of voluntary or charity work (helping others can be hugely healing)
- journal writing and Inner Child writing and drawing
- some kind of creative expression – making things with fabric, wood, or paper, or growing vegetables, or flowers, or whatever it is we do to relax.

In other words, it's living a "good life", having a loving and forgiving attitude, being creative, and balancing our necessary introspection with outward-looking compassion.

Key points

- "Shrugging it off" isn't the best thing for long-term healing and letting go.
- Buried emotions need to be understood and this can be painful.
- Acknowledging the depth of our hurt is crucial for long-term healing.
- Our different "attachments" that were developed in early childhood profoundly affect our responses and healing from difficult events, and our struggles to forgive.
- Being creative and caring for others can help to lighten the load.

Further reflections

"Each time you choose to deal with your feelings in healthy ways, to remove yourself from abusive situations, or take some time to get in touch with the memories, feelings, thoughts or body sensations associated with some past hurt, your inner strength increases. You add to this foundation of strength every time you make the choice to reclaim your feelings, each time you acknowledge and own what happened to you and how it has affected your life."

(Nancy J. Napier)

CHAPTER 22

Why is Forgiving So Hard Sometimes?

To study psychological trauma is to come face to face both with human vulnerability in the natural world and with the capacity for evil in human nature. To study psychological trauma means bearing witness to horrible events. When the events are natural disasters or "acts of God", those who bear witness sympathize readily with the victim. But when the traumatic events are of human design, those who bear witness are caught in the conflict between victim and perpetrator. It is morally impossible to remain neutral in this conflict. The bystander is forced to take sides.

It is very tempting to take the side of the perpetrator. All the perpetrator asks is that the bystander do nothing. He appeals to the universal desire to see, hear, and speak no evil. The victim, on the contrary, asks the bystander to share the burden of pain. The victim demands action, engagement and remembering.

(Judith Herman, a psychiatrist who has done considerable research into the effects of trauma)

183

The process of forgiving can be hard for some victims because the hurt was so huge that they have been traumatized – overwhelmed to the point where their body cannot cope. If they also had less than "secure attachment" during childhood, the problems can be even greater.

Presumably not everyone who has to endure, or see, some life-changing event is traumatized, but many are, and it is what happens to our bodies during that trauma that is the subject of this chapter.

Disintegration of self

Barbara Glasson in her book *A Spirituality of Survival: Enabling a Response to Trauma and Abuse* writes about the "disintegration of self" and what I've heard other people call "this awful disorientation" – both expressing exactly what it feels like to have endured trauma (only some of the time now, for me).

Sufferers of post-traumatic stress disorder (PTSD) can find they don't quite fit into the world – there is so much that is totally inexplicable that we can feel alienated from everything – alone in a strange and dangerous world where it is almost impossible to feel a sense of peace. Sometimes it's necessary for us to live in our own "alternative universe". I spent most of my childhood and teenage years in a fantasy world.

Our behaviour can look strange, and it's hard for people to understand such things as an adult being totally freaked out by something that seems innocuous – loud music, or some sound with a heavy regular beat, or some smells. I can't cope with one well-known men's deodorant; I degenerate into a trembling mass of jelly – not great on a London bus trying to get to work.

Hard to understand

When I'm working with groups of people on responding well to survivors of abuse, when I try to explain this "disintegration of self" I can see some people's eyes glaze over. They haven't got a clue what I'm talking about – and this is perfectly understandable because the symptoms of PTSD are hugely varied, some of them unique to PTSD. These are often muddled up with other symptoms; for example, depression problems such as being frightened to go out of the house, feeling suicidal, or feeling so dead inside that nothing makes sense any more.

I think, like depression, or bereavement, PTSD is one of those things you have to experience yourself if you are to understand it in any depth. But second best is to accept that this "disintegration of self" affects everything about a person's life – including forgiving.

Doing nothing

Judith Herman's book *Trauma and Recovery: The Aftermath of Violence – from Domestic Abuse to Political Terror* is most definitely worth reading if you want to understand more about trauma, and in her quote at the start of this chapter, she is saying that it is much easier for onlookers to do nothing when someone is in some deep pain and struggling to forgive. This is a very important factor when we are supporting someone struggling with forgiving.

The glib "just forgive", or "forgive and forget" plays into the hands of perpetrators because:

- the event will be dropped
- the effects on the victim minimized, and
- the whole incident will be forgotten – by everyone except the victim.

What the victim needs is time to talk, to share, to heal. But, Judith Herman maintains, that can only happen through human contact. Commanded to "just forgive" cuts the victim off from help – from human compassion – leaving them with a huge burden that can become overwhelming.

Again, I'm not talking here about hurt people who are determinedly seeking revenge. That is likely to end in even more long-term pain. I'm talking of people who are so hurt that forgiving is at the moment impossible, or who over time struggle to put down their burdens, only to find that this huge and complex task defeats them, leaving them depressed and anxious – and sometimes, sadly, surrounded by people insisting that forgiving is easy, further removing the hurt person from the help they so much need.

> The only thing necessary for the triumph of evil is for good men to do nothing.
>
> *(often attributed to Edmund Burke)*

A kind of denial?

The problem that victims of sexual abuse have is that sometimes they don't want to talk about it all that much, and others don't want to hear about it. This obviously creates a massive communication problem, and presumably something similar might be going on for other victims of trauma, such as torture, and those in families where someone has been murdered.

I think the problem here is that it's terribly difficult for anyone to have to take on board the evil things that human beings can inflict on others. Reading what happened during ethnic cleansing in various countries in the late twentieth century is unbearable. The details are so awful I want to shut them out of my head. In other words, I feel that it stops me coming alongside these victims as they struggle through their pain. I don't even want to think about it, and I wonder if this is a kind of denial.

But if we cannot bear the pain to be with someone suffering, that goes against what those who have studied trauma say is needed for a victim to recover. They need:

- lots of time to tell their story
- to be listened to attentively, and
- enabled to re-tell and re-tell their story until that terrible inner "disintegration of self" begins to piece itself back together.

Of course in most ordinary situations in life, usually there just isn't the time to do that – and doctors' understanding about trauma is a relatively new science. My early "help" from psychiatrists was thousands of antidepressants and tranquillizers!

Nowadays there might be better help than that. For those counsellors who are working alongside people who are trying to forgive, it is time and support that are needed if the person we are caring for is going to recover sufficiently to begin to let go and put down burdens of resentment.

Skilled help is really important, but as well as this, a listening friend or pastor can give more opportunity for the person to go over their story again. There is a health warning here though –

the role is to listen. Offering advice or platitudes can do more harm than good.

Time to talk

It's important for survivors of trauma who feel they can't talk about what happened to find the strength, gradually, to put the events into words. This might be helped by trying to write about it first; I found this a great help – and it's only me who saw my words unless I chose to share them with anyone.

There is evidence that talking can heal trauma. That's probably not a startling revelation because talking can be so healing in many human problems. So as we come alongside trauma victims, it's crucial to give time to talk before launching into issues about forgiveness.

> None of the churches I've belonged to have let me talk. They just wouldn't let me. "Don't keep going on about it," they kept saying. "You'll feel better if you move on and forget about it." But how could I forget? I so very much wanted just to talk.
>
> *(Wendy)*

Forgiving in our mind

However much we might want to forgive someone, if we have been traumatized, our mind may well want to forgive, we may desperately want to forgive because we feel we should, we might even insist we have forgiven, but our body still remembers and reacts.

This definitely isn't a sign that we haven't forgiven. The panics I sometimes get aren't a sign that I haven't forgiven my stepfather for sexually abusing me. They are signs that I was traumatized and my body is still trying to recover. My body is trying to catch up with my mind, and I'm trying to learn new patterns of behaviour.

When our body responds to something that reminds us of that huge hurt, our mind may race with angry and resentful thoughts. That's completely normal and to be expected. But, of course, we can be well on our way to forgiving the person who caused that hurt, or being able to let go to improve the quality of our own life. Our body is just trying to catch up.

But what if…?

What if there are daily reminders of the hurt? For example, for Louise there was the daily lack of money to buy ordinary things such as school uniform for her children, and some days she didn't eat anything other than bread so she could feed her children. They had to move out of their house to a small flat, the only place she could afford, but not ideal with four children. Putting her burden down in these circumstances is hard.

Anna dissociates most days (she loses time and goes into a catatonic state). She still self-harms. She is on so much medication she is like a zombie. She tells me that she still relives the trauma of being sexually abused by her brother.

Anna has daily reminders of the abuse and she says she wants to forgive, but her life is so chaotic – often weekly visits to the emergency room – that

> forgiving doesn't make any sense to me. I just can't get my head around what it means. It just makes me cry and I want to cut myself.

Anna says that she doesn't think she still blames her brother for what he did over so many years, but I've met with some people who do still blame those who hurt them. The trouble with blame is that it creates a cycle of resentment; people can find resentment begins to affect every aspect of their life. The more miserable they become, the more they want just to blame the people who hurt them. This makes them feel more hurt, trapped, and depressed, and so they spiral down into the pit of resentment. Don't go there! If this sounds like you, dump the blame! (There is more about strategies to lighten the load in chapter 27.)

Look from the point of view of the victim

Repeatedly in the stories in Section B we saw the powerful people, the vicars, counsellors and so on, seeing forgiveness as something "out there" – something you must do whatever the circumstances because it is something the church demands from its simplistic interpretations of Jesus' words.

But in my experience, forgiveness is something deep within me. I think this throws up a huge problem – that leaders don't always see forgiveness from the point of view of the victim. This is a point made by the Revd Dr Marie Fortune, an American pastor with considerable expertise in the area of violence against women and children:

> [Forgiveness] should be viewed from the experience of the
> victim and understood as only one aspect of the healing process.

It's the victims who are the vulnerable ones, and yet too often it is those vulnerable people who are viewed as the wrongdoers when they struggle to forgive.

Key points

- Trauma can lead to the "disintegration of self", and recovery from that is complex, and needs time.
- People who have been traumatized can need considerable time to recover enough to forgive.
- Healing from trauma is sped up by talking.
- In order to help we must listen rather than offer advice or tell people what to do – this can do more harm than good.

Further reflections

- Encouraging people to talk can help prevent the secrecy that often surrounds abuse.
- It is secrecy and silence that enables perpetrators to go on hurting people.

CHAPTER 23

It Takes Time to Forgive: Limbic Lag

In very simplistic terms, we have two parts to our brains. [This is not the same as the two hemispheres.] The first part is the neocortex. It is located in the front of the head and receives and stores information for decision making and remembering. The other part is called the limbic system, which controls all the automatic systems of the body and the emotions. Most importantly, the limbic system controls the survival responses, i.e., fight or flight and freeze. When you feel threatened, these protective responses tell you either to defend yourself or to run away or go numb. The limbic system doesn't have a memory like the neocortex. It doesn't know the difference between yesterday and 30 years ago, which explains why some of our childhood traumas still trigger us so powerfully today.

(Michael Dye)

As I've been trying to make sense of the muddle in my life as I recover from memories of early sexual abuse (which I had "forgotten" and which only returned in midlife) I've been talking to my friend Fran. This has been hugely important in my developing thinking about forgiveness.

Wow! That hurt!

Fran was working with me on trying to make sense of the emotional turmoil that I get into when my "difficult friend" puts me down, criticizes me in a very personal way, and generally dumps the bad things in her life onto me. It's incredibly uncomfortable being with this friend. Fran listened patiently to me describing conversations with this person and she suggested that one way to deal with the barbed comments would be to say to myself "Wow! That hurt!" when the comments come, let myself feel the hurt, then say to myself, "Now I'm letting it go."

This would all take place in a few seconds and, in theory, I'd be free of that hurt, the anger inside me would be less and I could move on with my friend. It sounded so easy. "Wow! That hurt! Now I'm letting it go." Surely I could learn to do that?

But I realized that the one main problem with it for me would be that I simply wouldn't be able to say, "Wow! That hurt!" *at the time of the hurt.*

I don't "hear" that kind of thing until ages afterwards. I don't "feel" hurts as they arise – I tend to go into a kind of numbness whenever anything even remotely close to conflict arises. I think this probably arose from me responding to conflict as a child by freezing rather then the flight or fight response that I learned about in biology at school, as I said earlier. So now my body has this habit and I freeze when my friend criticizes me.

Limbic lag

Some people call this time gap between the event and our understanding and feeling of it "limbic lag". What that means is that we may be physically aware of what happened – in other words, we may well have a memory of the event – but our emotions simply haven't yet caught up with our physical body.

We might be able to say the words, "It was awful!" but actually our feelings aren't touching what we can say with our rational mind. For example, I miscarried several babies in my twenties and thirties, and each time I thought I was fine. I'd dealt with the pain. But when I ran my first marathon aged sixty, I noticed two women in front of me who had "we are running for our babies we never held" written on their backs.

I fell apart. I cried uncontrollably, but I knew what was happening – I was at last feeling the real pain of that loss of our babies. It was limbic lag. My limbic system took over thirty years to catch up with my memories. (Not everyone needs that amount of time!)

Limbic lag and letting go

This time gap between the hurting event and us becoming aware of our true emotions about it – the "Wow! That hurt!" bit – shows us that if we aren't in touch with our feelings, how can we know what it is that we have to forgive? Yes, we could say the words "I forgive", and even mean them most sincerely, but for "deep" or "thick" forgiving, we need at some point to face our inner world and our burden of deeply entrenched emotions *that we aren't really aware of*.

The awful boss who keeps having a go at us and makes our life hell is hurting us as an adult. But what is connecting that bullying to earlier buried memories? To say, "I forgive my boss because she's clearly a power crazy, immature idiot" may not quite deal with all that is going on in my emotional life that is a hangover from childhood, or from a traumatizing event in adulthood.

My defensive barrier

So going back to Fran and her "Wow! That hurt! Now I'm letting it go", I began to see that doing this quick letting go was something I was going to have to work at. I would like to feel the stabbing comments from my "difficult friend" at the time she says it.

But I can't.

It's as if I have this defensive barricade around me so that even with intrusive, obviously hurtful things being said, although I remember them, I don't actually feel anything at the time. Clearly, what I needed to work on was allowing myself to feel things during conversations and meeting with people.

But that is mega-scary! It feels so unsafe. I know I'm a million times better at it than years ago. The limbic lag has gone from a few decades to a few weeks or days. But it isn't yet at nil time lag and this is likely to be a factor in letting go of our bad resentments.

Safe or dangerous?

In our ordinary life, when things happen to us, our limbic system sorts these events into either safe or dangerous. If something is seen as dangerous because of past trauma, the limbic system reacts by seeking out behaviour that enabled survival in the past – perhaps anxiety or depression. Michael Dye says that our limbic system can "create a focused craving for behavior that has been associated with survival" in our past experience. This craving can keep us focused on that behaviour until we get less stressed. In other words, we can get "addicted" to certain survival behaviour patterns.

To be free of stress, Anna on page 189 cuts herself. That's her addiction for survival. Many people retreat into depression to reduce stress – I'm one of them. Others resort to drugs, alcohol, food and sex to numb their emotions.

Probably everyone has survival mechanisms – they are crucial to managing life. But when we have ones that are overdeveloped and actually get in the way of us healing, then we're in trouble.

We just can't process it

I am writing this chapter in 2011 when the bomb and shootings in Norway are on the television news. Many of the victims are describing what they went through. Although some of them are in tears, the interviewer comments to a psychiatrist that some of the young people seem much calmer than we might expect. The doctor says something like this:

> Human beings just can't process this amount of information, so they can be calm initially, but as the weeks go by, people will start to see the enormous impact of an event like this.

The doctor went on to say that many of those in the two incidents, both victims and rescue workers, would experience post-traumatic stress disorder, despite being given counselling at the time. He explained that human bodies are just designed this way. The initial calm gradually changes as we process what happened to us and see the implications of the traumatic events. He said there is a need for long-term counselling to help people to process how their inner world has responded to the trauma.

How do we get beyond limbic lag?

If adults can need long-term counselling after trauma, it's easy to see that a traumatized child is also likely to have long-term issues that need sorting if they are going to learn not to retreat into their usual behaviour that numbs their feelings.

We have picked up "lies" from the earlier trauma – the "lies" I was told and believed were that I was useless and hopeless and deserved to be just a punchbag. To get beyond my limbic lag I need to challenge those beliefs and believe that I matter as a person and that I don't deserve to be treated badly.

However, it was much easier just to resort to depression or binge eating because if I did challenge the beliefs I had overwhelming anxiety. But the more I learned to challenge the old behaviour and thoughts, the stronger I got. Now (sometimes!) I see that I don't always need to go back to my old behaviour when the triggers from the past arise. I see that I survive without resorting to depression or food. The theory is that the more I realize I survive without this addictive behaviour, the better I will get and the limbic lag gets reprogrammed.

As we go through this process we get nearer to being able to forgive with meaning. We get more in touch with our emotions. (More about emotions in chapter 26.)

Forgiving is a process

Just as we need our daily bread, so we need our daily determination not to burden ourselves with our old behaviour, our negative thoughts and resentments, because these can make our journey through life even harder.

And this daily process can take varying amounts of time. Some need ten months. Some need ten years. We must not put a time limit on it. We need to remember Gee Walker's "every day".

If forgiving is a process (most people seem to believe this) then it makes a nonsense of saying, "If you don't forgive, God won't forgive you!" because, as Anthony Bash points out, how far through the process do you need to be to be forgiven by God? It doesn't make sense, because all of us are in that day-to-day process in some way. We all need to put down those annoying little burdens – those little irritations that we need to dump on a daily basis.

The fact is, as the doctor in Norway said after the bomb and the shootings, it takes people time to process big events. This isn't because they are

- bad forgivers
- bad people
- disobeying God
- "heading for hell".

It is because they are hurt people who need

- time to start to feel safe enough to face what happened
- time to process the horror they have experienced.

They have some kinds of difficulties in turning trauma into inner peace. And further burdening them with "You must forgive, or else…" just compounds their problems. God's love is much bigger and more expansive than this narrow and harsh view.

Key points

- Limbic lag is an important factor in the time some people need to process what has happened to them.
- For our healing to be "deep" we need to allow ourselves time to work out what our real feelings are.
- Talking is a crucial part of healing and it needs time.
- It doesn't matter how long we take to let go or forgive. It's a process and just being on the journey is enough.
- Forgiving is a daily process.

Further reflections

"I believe that unarmed truth and unconditional love will have the final word in reality. This is why right, temporarily defeated, is stronger than evil triumphant."

(Martin Luther King, Jr)

CHAPTER 24

Forgiving Ourselves and God

Reconciliation with God always comes as a discovery, not as an achievement.

(David W. Augsburger)

Forgiving isn't always about those who have hurt us. In my various conversations with people, many talked of their struggles to forgive themselves.

Often this is because people want to forgive but still feel hurt and angry. Or they are told they must forgive and they feel some shame that their feelings are still all over the place despite wanting to forgive, or at least let go. This apparent inability to control personal feelings can cause a loss of self-esteem. It can feel as though life is out of control. We blame ourselves for our weakness, and our feelings of guilt can be overwhelming and debilitating, causing more anxiety and making the forgiving process even more complex and difficult.

I was writing the first draft of this chapter when Lewis Hamilton, the Formula One driver, was said to have colluded with some lie his team told officials about an incident in an Australian Grand Prix, only to be found out – and on television. His face showed his shame as he had to admit that he'd gone along with the lie. I knew that he would have to learn to forgive himself.

Shame is powerful

Shame can build up so easily. The small child told off for spitting couldn't know that spitting out toothpaste is OK, but spitting at a person, even if they have just spat at you and hit you, isn't acceptable. How would a small child know that? She can't – and she is told off by an adult, and shame takes hold. "I'm bad," she says to herself.

Apparently the most common reason that people get depressed and need counselling is low self-esteem. This sense of our own worthlessness can grow from our sense of shame in childhood, and it is made into a huge problem if we experience any kind of abuse – bullying and name-calling included.

A positive dimension of the feeling of shame is that it shows us that for some reason we are not comfortable with ourselves, or in the presence of others – and opens the possibility of dealing with that. But much more often, our sense of shame is destructive in our inner world, making us feel worthless. But we aren't. We are valuable human beings, loved by God.

Unconditional love

This is why it's crucial to love our children unconditionally and to be clear when we tell them off that it is what they have done that we disapprove of – not who they are as a person. Hopefully that will prevent shame taking hold in them.

Presumably everyone does things they wish they hadn't, and don't do things they wish they had. This is where our need to forgive ourselves becomes important, otherwise our sense of shame can become too heavy a burden to bear, and with that added burden we are not usually in a position to be able to dump our heavy load.

Accepting who we are

Forgiving ourselves is a self-acceptance, saying something like: "Yes, I know I have failings. But that's OK. So does everyone. But God loves me so I'm going to focus on that love and learn to love and care appropriately for myself and for others."

There was a time when I thought "loving myself" was terrible – something I shouldn't do. But I learned that was adding to my heavy burden. I needed to love and accept myself, as Jesus put it when he talked about loving our neighbour *as ourselves*.

I was hugely affected by watching the film *American History X* when one of the characters says:

What have you done today to make your life better?

At first I thought that a bit selfish, but when I reflected on it I realized it contained a gem of an idea – something that is at the heart of living a contented and burden-free life – doing things to make our lives better. In that way we will be able to journey through life more easily, and make the lives of those around us more joyful.

Regretting what we did

Diana (chapter 5), who didn't realize her husband was also abusing the children, told me how bad she felt about insisting her children forgive their father. "That must have hurt them so much," she said to me. "I was quite wrong to say that."

Misjudging something and getting it wrong is part of everyone's life – part of the human condition. But a really harmful aspect following trauma is our tendency to change that blame and regret into self-punishment. Learning to dump that self-blame is a fundamental part of putting down our load of inner confusion.

A turning point

Susan Shooter, in her important book about how survivors of abuse relate to God talks of "a turning point" as we eventually acknowledge that seeing ourselves as evil isn't the true picture. Below, she quotes Suzanne Sgori; I've put Sgori's words in italics:

> [This] turning point ... is *an immensely freeing process* in which a survivor *gives permission to [the] self to end self-punishment*. Paradoxically, even though victims have no objective need to be forgiven for an offence which was not theirs, this stage [of giving permission to end self-punishment] is crucial. The coping mechanism which helped victims manage the anxiety of having had no control by mentally framing themselves as evil, contaminated and damaged is now being relinquished. Survivors invariably become "self punishers" [and this turning point brings to an end] behaviours which punish the self for being fallible and weak.

Forgiving God

As well as needing to forgive ourselves, some people I talked to were feeling that they needed to forgive God. I can sense what they mean, though I don't feel this myself. But others were horrified when I voiced the idea that some people needed to forgive God! It's apparently anathema to some – because, they say, God can do no wrong. But I think if we have been deeply hurt by some "act of God", there can be a need for us to work out in our own head why we think that God seems to allow this kind of suffering.

I have no idea how to handle the idea that bad things happen. Some writers can be so blasé about God apparently "allowing" a child to be sexually abused, and so on – these books make hideous reading. I don't know why God doesn't intervene to stop so much awfulness. To me, our world seems so totally inexplicable and ambiguous – but also utterly beautiful.

God in the Dark

Recently I read a most astonishing book called *God in the Dark* by Peter Longson, where the author reflects on his own and his family's responses to their daughter being sexually abused as a child, then raped as a young adult. Longson grapples with the kind of trite nonsense that some people said, such as "God was there with her", causing even more pain to the grief-stricken family.

I recommend this book if you are confused by why God seems to "let bad stuff happen to good people". It's a beautiful, poetic book and Longson's working out of his bewilderment makes satisfying reading. I can't possibly do justice to it in my book. There aren't "answers". But God's willingness to come to earth to suffer with us is something that I feel is important when I can't cope with life. I'm not alone.

I don't know why the loveliest of people die far too young from cancer, but when we weep in our pain and grief, it helps me to think that God is weeping too.

It's a wonderful world

What would our world be like if it was a pain-free zone and wasn't our cooling globe? No sea or rivers in case we drown. No gravity in case we drop something on our foot or fall off a mountain. No wind in case it blows trees down and we are crushed. No clouds in case there is lightning that strikes someone dead. No sun in case we burn. No fire. No suffering. No death.

I can't imagine a world like this. I like our beautiful world although it is full of risks and tragedy. Of course I wish that children didn't die of leukemia. I have no answer for that. Our world is just too ambiguous for me to understand.

Our freedom

God didn't make us like robots that just have to obey their master. We have freedom – we can love God and those around us, or choose not to. I think God gives our wonderful world to have some "freedom" as it cools from the origins of the universe. So there are unpredictable events – "acts of God", as insurance companies call them.

I know what I've written isn't an answer, but for me, our freedom in a risky world makes enough sense. (Do read Peter Longson's book if you want a much more coherent argument about "the problem of pain".)

Stronger people

One of my ways of seeing suffering is that it can tend to make us stronger people. It's not that working our way through pain is "good". It's that we could allow ourselves to become "better" people in the sense of having inner strength because of working through our difficulties. No one could have written *God in the Dark* without having been devastated. Now that book could help others who are confused – and angry with God.

> Forgiving is what love does … "Not to forgive," says Tom Wright, "is to shut down the faculty in the innermost person, which happens to be the same faculty that can receive God's forgiveness. It also happens to be the same faculty that can experience real joy and grief. Love bears all things, believes all things, hopes all things, endures all things." [Tom] is speaking of forgiving others, but I think the principle applies to our direct relationship with God. If I cannot forgive [God], maybe I cannot be forgiven. If I cannot forgive [God], maybe I slowly die.
>
> *(Peter Longson)*

The mystery

Yes, life is a mystery in many ways, but for me, faith is about keeping going anyway, despite that. Faith is the trust that God is holding on to us in spite of our uncertainties. I feel sure that we learn important aspects of contented living as we try to overcome our difficulties. If we let our hardships teach us, we can learn to be "better" human beings, with more empathy, and learn to lighten the load of those around us.

Try not to get in too much of a rage with those who say we'll look back on all our troubles and be "glad of them"!

Key points

- We need to learn to forgive ourselves to release us from a destructive sense of shame and guilt.
- Releasing ourselves from our self-punishment is an important turning point in our recovery from trauma.
- It's hard to answer the mystery of why we suffer.
- God weeps with us.
- If we allow our suffering to teach us, we can use that in creative ways to unburden ourselves and help those around us.

Further reflections

"Where is God when it hurts?

"He has been there from the beginning, designing a pain system that, even in the midst of a fallen world, still bears the stamp of his genius and equips us for life on this planet.

"He transforms pain, using it to teach and strengthen us, if we allow it to turn us towards him."

(Philip Yancey)

CHAPTER 25

Can We Define Forgiveness? The Forgiveness Umbrella

Many writers make clear that forgiveness can take many different forms. For example, Anthony Bash speaks about "forgiveness*es*", which makes trying to define forgiveness quite difficult. What does forgiveness involve when we have experienced what Stephen Cherry calls an "outrageous atrocity"? Each person is unique; each story is different. So I think it's probably best to think of forgiveness as an "umbrella term". I want in this chapter to clarify what I think belongs under the umbrella and what doesn't (see diagram).

- responding to moral wrongdoing

- dumping bad resentments

- keeping away from revenge

- seeking justice

- not holding grudges

- working through the stages of forgiving

- learning to dump blame

- taking back our personal power

- basking in God's love and forgiveness

- searching for truth

- developing a merciful and forgiving attitude

- can involve reconciliation

- clarifying our feelings

- learning to deal with anger

- praying for those who hurt us

- forgiving those who apologise sincerely

- healing

- letting go

What isn't under the umbrella?

Forgiving isn't:

- a cure for all painful situations
- condoning what was done – not "he came from an abusive home so we mustn't blame him". No! While we want to be sensitive and generous to people, what he did was wrong
- saying it's OK what that person did. No! If it was wrong, it isn't OK
- letting someone "off the hook"
- pretending that everything is all right really
- saying that is does not matter
- diminishing in any way the degree of hurt that took place
- something that means we should no longer search for justice
- some kind of legal pardon meaning the offender will escape punishment by the state
- believing that wrong and hurt can be simply forgotten
- anything to do with threats about whether God will continue to love us or not.

What is under the umbrella?

Forgiveness involves:

- a response to moral wrongdoing, to something wrong in a relationship
- putting our burdens down, gradually, over time

- letting go of retaliation, hatred and destructive resentment
- keeping away from revenge
- letting go of grudges
- learning to dump blame
- healing for hurt emotions and painful memories
- a series of stages to work through, or "emotional threads" to untangle
- taking back our personal power
- searching for truth
- developing a merciful and forgiving attitude
- learning to deal with our anger and not let it become destructive
- searching for a contented life where we can achieve our goals
- basking in God's love and forgiveness
- finding creative ways to respond to those who hurt us
- praying for those who have wronged us
- working together with other hurt people, finding strength in each other and seeking that peace we see in others who have put down more of their burden than we have
- an apology and repentance from the perpetrator (by no means always)
- healing for the perpetrator (after they have apologized)
- sometimes it can mean that a relationship is restored – but not always (for example, where there has been sexual abuse it would be very important not to trust the perpetrator, even if they say sorry).

Sometimes forgiveness can involve some kind of restitution, but that seems quite rare. There are occasions when a victim takes a perpetrator to court and gets financial compensation, but amongst the many survivors of abuse that I know, I don't think any of them have had that kind of restitution. Most haven't even had an apology.

But forgiving can be:

- very difficult indeed and impossible for some (at the moment – and we would do well not to put limits on that by saying "never", because we don't know what the next phase of our life will bring)

- complicated because we are exploring both our inner world and trying to make sense of why someone would hurt us so badly

- mysterious and difficult to "find", made worse when we are put under pressure and threatened

- inappropriate in some cases

- *but also:* peaceful and creative; it makes us want to sing and dance with delight at our beautiful world and the friendship of others we have drawn close to in our pain, and the love of God which surrounds us.

So what is forgiving?

Forgiving is a very slippery concept. We think we've got a grasp on it but then, like a bar of soap in the shower, it slips away from us. It's an umbrella term with many different levels and perspectives, from Anthony Bash's "thick" forgiveness to a very loose kind of letting go in order to make our lives better when that is all we can do in our circumstances.

So forgiveness, like love, can be hard to define – but we can recognize it when we see it.

And one thing most writers agree on is that all forgiveness ultimately comes from God. Forgiveness is a gift, freely given. A gift, *freely* given!

Key points

- Forgiveness can be complex.
- It's helpful to see forgiveness as an umbrella term with lots of different aspects to it.
- Forgiveness is a gift from God.

Further reflection

"Keep your thoughts positive because your thoughts become your words. Keep your words positive because your words become your behaviour. Keep your behaviour positive because your behaviour becomes your habits. Keep your habits positive because your habits become your values. Keep your values positive because your values become your destiny."

(Mahatma Gandhi)

CHAPTER 26

The Forgiving Process: Untangling Some Threads

Teachers open the door, but you must enter by yourself.

(Chinese proverb)

Forgiving can be quite a complex idea, partly because it can be about so many different things. That is why the previous chapter talked about "forgiveness**es**".

The Linn family, in their wonderfully titled book *Don't Forgive Too Soon* suggest that forgiving has five stages:

- Denial
- Anger
- Bargaining
- Grief
- Acceptance.

Interestingly, these are the same stages that people seem to go through when they know they are terminally ill, or experience a significant bereavement.

And to my surprise, I went through those same five stages earlier this year when I had a really bad knee injury and couldn't run for three months. Going through the stages of various different feelings with my knee fascinated me, so there must be something about these five stages that is basic to a wide range of human experiences – maybe they are fundamental to facing difficulties in our lives.

The stages are unlikely to be straightforward though. Life is much more complex than talking about stages might imply because we loop around and back, some days feeling back to square one and others feeling more hopeful.

Post-traumatic stress

When forgiving is coupled with recovery from trauma, there are going to be other complications, and in her important book, psychiatrist Judith Herman identifies three stages in recovery from trauma:

> Recovery unfolds in three stages. The central task of the first stage is the establishment of safety. The central task of the second stage is remembrance and mourning. The central task of the third stage is reconnection with ordinary life.

Twelve stages or threads to untangle

So I have tried to weave the five stages of forgiving with the three stages of recovery from trauma and I've come up with a possible twelve "threads to untangle" as we go through the process. (But remember that the process and the circumstances will be different for everyone.)

Before I get to the twelve stages, there are three important points:

- Understanding our feelings as we go through the process is crucial – but very difficult, and there is more about feelings in chapter 27.

- It's crucial to note within these stages of recovery the inevitability of victims becoming self-punishers, and this seems to be particularly true after childhood sexual abuse. We hate ourselves. "It must have been my fault," I said to myself for decades. And moving away from that damaging attitude is part of those stages of recovery. For me, the process of recovery was complex and frustrating. But I was amazed to discover that Judith Herman's "stages" were what I went through – in a very roundabout and messy way. But I am still something of a self-punisher! So any stages need to be seen as a guide to help us to analyze what's going on, not something set in stone.

- Although I've written these stages as a list, remember that the process of forgiving isn't at all a series of steps where we start at stage one and move on in a linear way. I used to think of it more like a helix in which we have to keep revisiting the same old things over and over again, but now I think even that makes the changes in our lives sound a bit too tidy.

To be honest, my own process of forgiving seems to be much more like a ball of wool when it's been played with by two kittens! For example, I'm sure I've forgiven the people who hurt me, but I still have a powerful need to feel safe – Judith Herman's first stage. And I also don't see myself as at the end of the process of forgiving. As I keep saying, Gee Walker got it just right when she said "every day… oh… every day".

So this process of letting go or forgiving seems to me to be more about us trying to untangle threads. As we try to find an end, perhaps understanding our anger, we find a dozen more tangled knots that we need to work on.

The threads or dimensions of forgiving

1. The event and denial

"It hasn't happened."

"I'm not going to admit that I'm hurt. I'll be fine."

"I probably deserve it."

"I can pull myself together."

We may feel numb – "dead inside".

We might take weeks, even years, to reach the stage where we can allow ourselves to feel angry and accept what has happened.

Traumatized victims may well be so unable to accept what has occurred that they "forget" the event/s. What has happened is too overwhelming – so all our body can do is freeze and not allow the memory to come out.

2. Breaking down in tears and rage

As the numbness wears off, for those struggling with post-traumatic stress there is a searching for somewhere to feel safe. Without some sense of safety, we cannot move on to a point where we can acknowledge the truth of what happened.

When something happens that triggers our memory of the event, we may well find ourselves overreacting to some small incident, and this gives our inner anger a chance to break out so that we can see it.

Our memories that were "forgotten" can burst into our consciousness in uncomfortable ways: flashbacks, nightmares and "body memories" when we can even get intense physical pain. Now we have "remembered", our life can become even more difficult.

Our experiences can be a confused mess of tears, anger and a horrible loss of a sense of safety.

"No way am I turning the other cheek. You mess with me like this and I'll get back at you."

"My life is in ruins because of what they did."

"Why can't I have justice?"

Remember that this anger is normal and not wrong. Wanting revenge is normal too, but it really is best not to carry out our ideas. Usually our wish for revenge will diminish.

Life can become chaotic with so many fears and phobias that normal life is impossible. The need to feel safe can rule our lives.

What happened to me at this point was that I went back into denial for years: *"It didn't happen. I'm such a bad person. I'm making it up."*

Depression and/or anxiety/phobias can become problematic and need medical help. Suicidal thoughts are common at this stage.

3. Anger seen alongside forgiving

"Why should I forgive? Look what they did to me. I want justice, not forgiveness. They don't deserve to be forgiven."

"How do I get rid of this much anger? Will forgiving help?"

"I will try to stop myself thinking up revenge."

"I don't want my life to go on being this awful but I don't know how to stop it."

We realize that we are carrying a huge burden, but might be confused about what this burden actually is. We can be unclear about the long-term effects we are experiencing and still trying to "pull ourselves together".

Alongside our anger, rather oddly, can come the familiar numbness: *"I feel nothing."* This internalized anger can turn to depression. Anxiety can still be a huge problem and needing to be safe can feel the most important thing in the world.

4. Starting to bargain and grieve

We're likely to want to retell our story many times to anyone who will listen, and this can be profoundly healing. This need to retell is a crucial part of "remembrance and mourning". Judith Herman identifies our need to "reconstruct our story" so that traumatic memory is transformed.

"Well, I might forgive them if they…"

"These are my conditions if you want me to forgive."

"I'm waiting for them to apologize."

"I feel so devastated. My old life has disappeared and it is never likely to come back again."

"I can never get my childhood back. They took my innocence for their

own pleasure. If it hadn't happened I'd be happier/in a better job/be able to be a better parent."

"They say they didn't do it. All I can do is sit on the sofa and weep."

This stage of "mourning traumatic loss" can be happening alongside us beginning to see *"It wasn't all my fault."* This freeing process is crucial, but can take years – it's the part of the process where we learn not to be self-punishers (eventually!).

We might be surrounded by people wanting us to forgive. But we are overloaded with grief. We might begin to feel guilt that we feel we can't forgive. We realize that our burden is getting heavier and now we know that burden includes guilt. This can contribute to us feeling unsafe which is likely to send us spiralling down into fear and chaos.

We might still want justice (quite rightly).

5. Wondering how forgiveness works

We might wonder what would need to happen inside us to take out our inner pain.

"I don't know how to forgive. It feels impossible and I just can't do it."

"I feel too angry to forgive."

"They haven't said sorry, so I don't see why I should forgive."

"I can't stop the flashbacks. They come at me so unpredictably. I just want to be at home under my duvet where I feel safe. I can't make any sense of what it would mean to forgive. It feels as if I'd be saying that what they did to me was OK."

We might still want justice (of course). The burden can be intolerable.

6. Realizing we can start to let go

"I suppose I could try to stop thinking about it all the time."

"I'm not going to forgive them. I can't. But I'm going to 'let go' for my own mental health."

We might realize that if we can get on with our lives, we can build new relationships and make other attempts to reconnect with ordinary life. We are likely still to be struggling with low self-esteem – still trying to "forgive ourselves" for what happened. (Yes, I know there was no fault on our part, but forgiving ourselves still seems to be crucial.)

We might still be striving for justice – and that isn't wrong. And we are likely still to be grieving for what we lost and the ways in which our life has been shattered.

7. Letting go but not forgiving

By now we might be showing signs of gritting our teeth and being more determined to fight for what we think is right.

"I try to let go, but I have to keep working at it."

"I can never forget this so I suppose that means I can't forgive."

"I still want justice and I'm going to sue them."

"I want a public enquiry so this never happens to another family."

We might be confused at the tension between forgiving and getting justice. To get justice we might need to fight for years – even decades.

We still need to tell and retell our story.

8. Realizing we are still carrying the burden of rage and memories

"I thought I was letting go but the memories of it all scream into my mind when I'm not expecting it."

"I thought I was on the way to forgiving but my feelings show me that I haven't forgiven at all."

We might start/continue to see ourselves as a bad person and be worried about how we seem to have to keep revisiting things we thought we had let go.

The need to feel safe all the time is likely still to be there, sometimes very powerfully if we feel threatened in certain situations.

9. Falling apart

"I thought I was getting better but I can't cope with any of this. I feel guilty I can't forgive."

"It's all my fault. I'm a bad person. I'm falling apart. I can't work. I can't look after my family."

"I'm utterly depressed and I know depression can be anger turned in on yourself. I can't manage my anger so I must suppress it."

People are likely still to be telling us that it all happened so long ago that we must forget about it. But we cannot do that, so the burden gets greater. The grief at times can be overwhelming. Christians around us might be telling us that no one with faith has a nervous breakdown and that we need to pray more. (My strategy to deal with people like this is to keep away from them.)

10. Beginning to put the burden down some of the time

"I'm gradually letting go. Some days are much better than others but I know I'm less depressed now."

"I'm starting to see it wasn't all my fault."

"I'm still confused about what forgiveness feels like."

"I do want to forgive but I'm not sure I should. That might make it look as if what they did was nothing."

"I don't know what the future holds."

We might begin to see that our life can get better. We recognize that we need to put the burden down and some days we can manage to do that. On other days we can feel our anger and grief again and still, understandably, might want justice. Feeling safe can continue to be an issue.

11. Putting the burden down most of the time

"I'm going to try to help others who went through the same experience."

"I can see I'm never going to get justice, so I need to let that go."

"I'm so much happier. I feel good about myself. I see it wasn't my fault."

"Even if they won't apologize I'm going to let it all go to stop myself getting bitter and twisted."

We can feel a sense of release and freedom. We might try to move towards reconciliation. (Maybe! Sometimes reconciliation isn't appropriate, e.g. where we cannot trust a sex offender not to abuse. Even if they say sorry, that doesn't mean they will overcome their deep urges.)

12. Free of the burden

"I'm happier now than I have ever been."

"I can see that loving my family and friends is more important than demanding my rights to justice."

"I feel strong in myself. I know who I am and I'm determined to have as good a life as I possibly can and love those around me."

"I'm giving up my right to have justice and some kind of compensation."

(NB This last one is only for some people. I accept that some campaigners might never get to that position, and that's OK because seeking justice is important.)

We recognize we might never reach this stage and that is OK too.

As we get older and closer to death we might see that whatever has happened in our life, God goes on loving us just the same.

Even if we can't let go or forgive, God loves us.

God's love is not dependent on us forgiving.

Everyone's journey is unique

It's important that we always see our working our way towards putting down the things that burden us as something unique to ourselves, and if you don't feel you fit into what I have described, that's OK. Sometimes it can be hugely difficult to put a label on our feelings and that's OK too.

The important thing is not to get stuck, but instead to feel that we are making progress at dumping our burdens and starting to feel a sense of freedom. There is more about how we might set about dumping our burdens in chapter 27 where I suggest some strategies for letting go.

Key points

- The process of letting go can be confusing and complex, although we can sometimes identify some stages or threads.
- Our processes through letting go and forgiving are likely to be unique to us and to our story.

Further reflection

As we try to untangle the threads of the forgiving process, so we move closer to a balanced view of life (chapter 17), and experience more of the fruit of God's Spirit, which Paul describes as:

- love
- joy
- peace
- patience
- kindness
- generosity
- faithfulness
- gentleness
- self-control.

(Galatians chapter 5 verses 22 and 23)

SECTION D

In this section I explore the idea that we might well be further through the forgiving process than we think.

There are strategies for putting down the load – suggestions for how to heal from trauma, and positive ways forward to heal from our past life and the pressures we might feel under to forgive when we are finding that difficult.

The concluding chapter is for those who have a role in supporting people who are struggling with putting down their burdens, and I make suggestions for ways in which we might make faith, and the church, a more positive and affirming part of our lives.

CHAPTER 27

Strategies to Lighten the Load

When I befriend my anger and use it creatively, it can save my life.

(Dennis Linn, Sheila Fabricant Linn, Matthew Linn)

This chapter focuses on aspects of dumping our load of emotional baggage, and understanding our feelings as we do so.

I puzzled for years over Victoria's words in chapter 1:

I wonder what we actually do when we forgive?

and it is these strategies that I think are the things we need to do.

I've developed them from talking with others, and from my own process of letting go, which was strongly influenced by some excellent psychotherapy when my life seemed totally out of control. Probably not all the strategies will fit with your circumstances, but I think it's our determination to dump our emotional baggage that is an important part of our process of moving towards letting go and healing.

Start with the easier things

Some aspects of recovery are easier than others, but I realize that some people reading this might decide that nothing is easy. However, we can work towards finding something that is *easier than some other things.* An ideal way to sort that out is to write about it in your journal.

If you are like me, thinking can go round and round in your head, getting louder and louder, more and more confusing, and one solution to this is to write, or draw, or paint, or find some other creative way of changing the confused thinking into coherent sentences or images.

This process of clarifying our thinking and feelings needs us to use our will, as I explored in chapter 16. We need to *want* to heal. We need to *want* our life to be better. But no amount of extreme effort alone will get us there. We need to bask in God's love and tell ourselves daily that all forgiveness comes from God.

The rest of these strategies are in no particular order: we are all different.

Healing of memories

Some years ago I was greatly helped by what was called a ministry of "healing of memories", that is, prayer that God would heal our damaged emotions. I think it is that healing process of getting beyond past pain that speeds along our letting go. As we

- meditate and pray
- take care to live a good healthy life
- gradually learn to let go of the hurt (usually with help, such as working at this list of strategies)

so we heal, our self-esteem becomes more healthy, we stop putting ourselves down and gradually lose our sense of shame.

Keeping our body healthy

There is evidence that we will have a stronger and more positive mental and spiritual outlook if our body is also healthy. Eating well can help us feel happier, so dump the junk! (That is not consuming too much "fast" or processed food that has additives, artificial sweeteners, corn syrup, trans fats etc. in it.) Taking exercise is a crucial part of the healing process. It doesn't matter what kind of exercise we do – dancing, walking, swimming, Zumba, or skipping will all help. The important thing is to find something you like so that you enjoy it and keep doing it. It might be excruciating at first. I used not to be able to run for two minutes. Now I can run marathons. Keep at it and you will get fitter. Exercise boosts our mood, so we feel more upbeat and positive.

We're further along than we think!

One astonishing thing I found with survivors of abuse was that they were almost always much further along the forgiving process than they thought they were. Just because we might still feel angry, or still be thinking about what happened, that doesn't mean we haven't started the process of letting go. So one strategy to lighten the load is to recognize how far we've already come.

We are starting to let go if we are

- not actively planning revenge
- feeling furious rage – but not taking that anger out on the person who hurt us, or anyone else
- throwing all our rage and confusion at God because we recognize that we are too upset to cope with it on our own

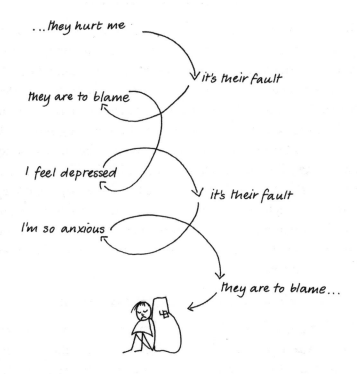

- recognizing that our anger is a part of the healing process; it means we are aware of how much we have been hurt and are able to be honest to ourselves about that, rather than denying the depth of the pain

- recognizing that keeping blaming someone is going to drag us down into more confusion and depression. Yes, in many circumstances the person was to blame. Yes, it shouldn't have happened. Yes, it was their fault. But we can get horribly stuck at that point and go on loading more and more stress and anxiety into our backpack. We

231

could go on saying "It's their fault!" for the rest of our lives. This would mean that we'd be allowing those who hurt us to go on ruining the rest of our life. (See "Taking back our personal power", later in this chapter). Dump the blame! Let it go. Don't risk getting caught in the spiral of resentment

- making serious attempts at dumping our negative thinking and resentments, and trying to find some level of managing our lives, despite what has happened. The more we try to cut negative thinking out of our lives ("I'm so hopeless, it's all their fault, what's the point in living?") the more our backpack will feel lighter. Identify that negative thinking. Then chuck it out

- seeking justice in a calm and mature way – haranguing people just makes them rush in the opposite direction. It might be that we need to recognize that in our situation we may never get justice, so plan a way forward despite that so that we don't become "bitter and twisted"

- working at not thinking about the awful situation and finding ways to counter this negative rumination with more life-affirming thoughts

- recognizing that it's OK to have "good resentment", e.g. searching for justice and trying to put right a wrong.

Further on in our journey we might find we are:

- praying for the person who hurt us – this is really tough, but we can angle our prayers towards the truth coming out (it has a way of doing that). Yes, there is likely to be anger in these prayers and a longing for justice (and maybe even a touch of hoping the people get their comeuppance, but be careful with that because it's a bit close to going back to hoping for revenge), but these prayers are at least us praying for the perpetrators – and keeping us focused on the fact that we need to keep handing the whole situation over to God. I think in some ways that it can be easier to ask God to forgive the person than it can be for us to forgive. It is God who will judge those who hurt us – not us

- starting to want the best for the person who hurt us – even if that means a spell in prison for them

- recognizing that we cannot change the past so it is best to put every effort into making the future the best that it can be in our situation. This might mean for us that we let go for the sake of our mental health (This is not selfish!)

- asking God to help us to have the will to consider putting our burden down on a daily basis – engaging with the idea that we are beginning a difficult process that is, as I keep saying, "every day… oh… every day"

- keeping aware that we could slip back into negative resentments unless we guard what we are thinking, and aim to find peace and contentment, despite it all

- recognizing that *we have let go* – and maybe this might lead us to start to consider thinking about calling that process "forgiving". (Although if we haven't had an apology, or for some other reason we don't think in our situation that it is appropriate to forgive, then accepting we have let go is a great step – with no reason to feel any guilt that this is what we think is right for us.)

So even if you only feel you are doing one or two of these things, I still think that you are in the process of letting go, or forgiving. Following a significant hurt, doing just one of these things on the list is brilliant.

Getting help

It's hard to get good therapy. It can be so expensive. Some of mine was free from the NHS and I am so grateful for that. It changed my life dramatically. So the first place to start is your GP, especially if you are depressed and anxious. (If your GP is hopeless then go to another one.)

I'm still taking antidepressants at the moment, and they make me feel well enough to face life – and have the ability, and the incentive to work at my thinking. I can write upbeat things in my journal and can feel that I'm making progress.

Dumping the victim

As we try to untangle the different threads of our hurts and let go, one crucial thing to dump is our sense of *being a victim* – almost allowing our victimhood to define our life. If we become "the person who was abused" or get labelled in some similar way, this is likely to add to our burdens because if we see ourselves as a victim, it's almost as if we have some role that we must go on preserving.

Accept that we need time

We need to recognize that there is likely to be a time lag between our experiencing some traumatic event and our being able to appreciate the impact of what happened on our inner life.

Even for people we might think of as "together" and "balanced and mature", this isn't necessarily an easy or quick process.

The process is particularly slow and tortuous for those abused in childhood, or those from dysfunctional families, or those who have been raped or tortured.

I'm not at all discounting the many books that tell of instant and dramatic forgiving and the ways in which those amazing transforming moments can totally change lives. But I think this kind of forgiving probably isn't how it is for many people. Unfortunately, those books, and some people's woolly interpretations of the Bible, alongside the experiences of some Christians' "instant forgiving", have fed into the belief that *this dramatic instant stuff is how it should be for everyone.*

For most people who have been deeply hurt, forgiving is a process, often involving eye-wateringly difficult years of costly and courageous trudging onwards. It can be back-breaking work. I hope in this book I'm clarifying what *could* happen.

Accept that it wasn't our fault

Traumatized people often can't connect up rational belief with what their inner world is telling them. We believe it was all our fault.

But this awful guilt is something we don't need to be carrying. Even if we are totally convinced that something was our fault, God still loves us. We are forgiven. We can pull that guilt out of our backpack and hurl it into the depths of the sea.

We are forgiven!

Working at dumping shame

This false guilt we feel can transform itself into one of the most powerful of human feelings – shame. Shame keeps us weighed down, feeling we don't matter as people.

I find it hard to dump my sense of shame, but I've been greatly helped by Lewis Smedes' book *Shame and Grace*. In a nutshell, what Dr Smedes says is that we need to allow ourselves to be loved and accepted by God as a special and valuable child of God. There is no need for us to feel shame, even if we have done something terrible. God is a God who forgives – and loves – unconditionally.

Working at understanding the load

It's important to be honest with ourselves about the depth of the hurt. It's the "disintegration of self" because of trauma that is so damaging. This can mean many aspects of our life are likely to be "all over the place". Our perceptions of reality can be a bit weird. For example, a lovely young woman came to see me because she was convinced that if she killed herself, her husband could remarry and get a better wife, and this person would be a better mother to her little girls. This is exactly how I felt years ago. At that time I was convinced I was right; I believed in it utterly. Now it sends fear down my body. I'm appalled at what I might have done in my suicide attempts.

Deep hurts can twist our perceptions of reality.

Wanting to keep carrying the load

We must look out for the danger of wanting to carry the load – although we may be totally unaware that is what we are choosing. Some of the people I've worked with around issues of helping survivors of abuse almost seem to be *choosing to keep their burdens*. Indeed, they seem worryingly attached to them.

Many people seem to find great meaning, when something happens to them or a loved one, in starting a campaign, or getting a public enquiry "so that no one ever has to suffer like we suffered". Isn't there the temptation to hang on to the burden, especially if we have made it our life's work to get justice?

I'm not talking here about those for whom any kind of forgiving is impossible; when the wrongdoer is dead so we can get no closure, or we know we will never get an apology, or the crime was so heinous we cannot believe it is ever possible to forgive.

I don't mean these personal views on forgiving; I mean the temptation to hang on to our hurts because we know where we are with them. The burden feels part of our life. We can't let it go.

It can feel far too scary to do that. *The burden has become part of who we are – our very identity as a person.*

This is dangerous ground.

We need courage

I know a few people who seem to give out the message "poor me, I need to be looked after" and for some, that's true. They do need lots of support. But I recognize in myself that I did that "poor me" for much too long. It was easier to keep being a bit feeble than to acknowledge that I had to dump that stuff. My life was now so much better that I could walk free, but that required me to be stronger and more courageous. It was very much easier to stay feeble!

Changing how we think

Psychologists estimate that we conduct a steady stream of internal conversation with ourselves amounting to around 300 words a minute. Just imagine if you could harness this unconscious stream of chatter and [turn it into] an opportunity for reprogramming yourself and giving yourself a good pep talk when you need it. Well, you can.

We know from research [into] this complex subject that negative thoughts produce negative emotions; they in turn lead to negative outcomes. But the reverse is equally true: positive feelings lead to high self-belief, confidence and positive results.

(*Paula Radcliffe*)

It sounds astonishing that we have 300 words a minute! But even if some of those are negative ruminations, learning not to think that way can have a dramatic and positive boost to our lives.

Cognitive behavioural therapy (CBT)

Therapy is expensive and sometimes difficult to find, but we can get access to effective CBT through books and online – and sometimes you can get this CBT through your GP. I've been working through a book (see the Resources at the back of this book) and I've found that helpful to keep a check on what's going on in my head.

CBT can help us *change our thinking*. This can cut down the negative messages we are giving ourselves and give us back some sense of personal power to feel that we are taking more control over our lives – we're not letting the person who hurt us go on hurting us, an absolutely crucial aspect of letting go.

We could say to ourselves:

- You are no longer a victim; you are a survivor.
- This is old stuff and you will feel much happier if you think about the goldfinches on the bird feeders instead.
- I'm *not* going to do this negative thinking.

Changing our thinking is challenging, and it involves acts of our will, but it has huge rewards.

Working at understanding our feelings

In chapter 26 I outlined the stages that we might go through as we learn to put down the load of feelings we might have, and as I've discussed these stages with people, it's interesting that

- They talk of being unable to identify their feelings and instead say they "feel confused".
- Some insist that they "just feel numb". "I feel nothing," a young man said when he was attacked, robbed, and badly injured in the 2011 riots in England.
- When we try to identify feelings, the main feeling people talk to me about is anger. So it's possible that anger is more easily identified than other feelings.

A crucial skill

It's absolutely essential that we learn to identify our emotions! It will give us a greater sense of our own empowerment and management of our life. Without being clear about our feelings we are likely to feel that when difficult events happen, we are just tossed about through circumstances in a random way. This can make us feel our life is out of control and that can be frightening – and feel horribly unsafe.

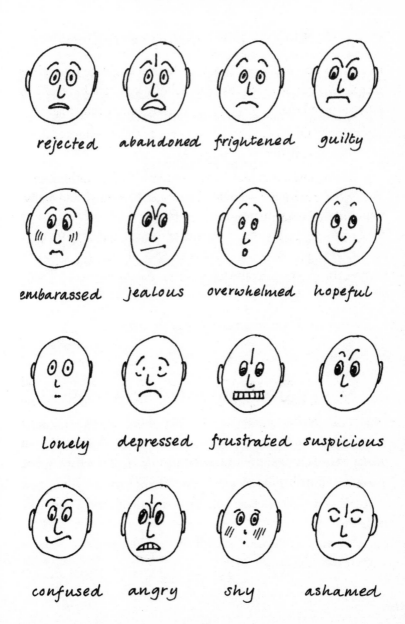

rejected   abandoned   frightened   guilty

embarassed   jealous   overwhelmed   hopeful

lonely   depressed   frustrated   suspicious

confused   angry   shy   ashamed

Look at the faces in the picture and try to identify how you are feeling today, or how you feel about what happened to you. It helps our confusion and numbness if we try to list our emotions, perhaps in our journal. As Nancy Napier says in *Getting Through the Day*, we get stronger every time we "reclaim our feelings".

Inner Child work

In chapter 21 I outlined some Inner Child activities that you might like to try. The power of the Inner Child work I did was to uncover some inner thinking and emotions that I didn't know about. This gave me more access to what it was that I had to forgive those who hurt me when I was a child. When we know what it is that hurt us, we will be more able to let it go.

> You must be the change you wish to see in the world.
>
> *(Mahatma Gandhi)*

Keeping a check on comforting rumination

There can be something comforting about our ruminations sometimes – going over and over more "scenes" and thinking about what we could have done. I find I also replay what I might do or say in the future when (I tell myself) I will be vindicated and everyone will see that nothing was my fault and I was right all along!

But this can become a habit that is likely to draw us away from reality and into fantasy.

Taking back our personal power

If we want to be free of that ghastly load we've struggled with for years, that determination not to let those who hurt us go on negatively influencing our life is very *very* important. This is where the decision to forgive can start with us letting go for our own mental health.

When we were hurt we lost personal power – we felt helpless. We need to take that power back in our lives. We need to learn that we are loved. We are valuable human beings. We matter and Jesus said that if anyone hurts one of God's little ones (us), it would be better for that person if they were thrown into the sea with a millstone round their neck (see e.g. Matthew chapter 18 verse 6).

If we take back our personal power we can learn to take more control in our lives, for example by being determined not to be a "doormat", or not going on blaming someone. Don't let those who hurt you go on ruining your life! Pull that rage and sense of powerlessness out of your backpack and dump it all on God.

Releasing the perpetrator

Many people pointed out during discussions with me that our letting go releases the person who hurt us. OK, we might initially not want to do that, but I think it is important to accept that it is God who will judge that person, not us.

Some people insisted that this releasing of the wrongdoer is crucial, and I think that's probably right; it's an important part of loving our enemies – Jesus was pretty hot on that. So even if all we can do is let go for our mental health, that's a good stage to get to – and we can leave the rest of the forgiving to God.

Working at having a forgiving attitude to life

Working at dumping what we can, when we can, needs us to be determined to keep our inner world a bad resentment free zone. I find this hard work. But I need to get this bad stuff out of my life in order to experience and enjoy God's love.

It's a theme throughout this book that it is God's love and forgiveness for us that enables us to develop a forgiving attitude. Remember that it is this forgiving attitude that identifies us as a Christian. We can still have a problem with the people who hurt us, but as we work at this forgiving attitude it's important that we are gentle with ourselves – self-acceptance is so important.

Relax! Stop worrying! I'm convinced that

- taking a walk in the park enjoying God's beautiful world, or
- doing something for someone else, or
- doing something else creative, and
- keeping our body healthy by eating well and exercising

is part of our working towards our forgiving attitude.

Allowing God to forgive and love us – just imagining those loving arms around us – will help us to be forgiving and loving people.

I love you

And finally, remember, as we say the Lord's Prayer we don't have to forgive in order for God to love us! It's not that God says: "You forgive first then I'll forgive you." NO!

It's "I love you, I love you, I *love* you! And the more you rest in that love and surround yourself with it, the more you will find you can put your burdens down. I'm the one who gives you the power to let go.

"My love is a completely free gift of grace and mercy. All you have to do is to want to have this free gift. Honestly! No strings attached! (Well, it would be great if you could love me back.)

"I love you. I accept you just as you are – don't listen to those who tell you otherwise!"

> Come to me, all you that are weary and are carrying heavy burdens, and I will give you rest. Take my yoke upon you, and learn from me; for I am gentle and humble in heart, and you will find rest for your souls. For my yoke is easy, and my burden is light.
>
> (Matthew chapter 11 verses 28–30)

Key points

- There are many strategies we can try that can help us to dump the emotional baggage that is stopping us feeling contented and at peace.
- As we experience God's love and forgiveness, so we can develop a forgiving attitude.

Further reflections

If we work at our mental health we will be more likely to be able to let go of bad resentments and anger. This is likely to be a long-term project.

"Forgiveness is not an answer or a quick fix. It is agony. However, it is not merely agony – it is healing agony."

(Stephen Cherry)

CHAPTER 28

For Supporters of People Who are Struggling with Forgiving

Why do Christians shoot their wounded?

(Dwight Carlson)

This chapter is for those who have some kind of supporting role for people who struggle with life and I want to make suggestions for when we find ourselves responding to a person who is finding forgiving difficult.

Dwight Carlson, in his book of the same title, expresses the problem exactly: Why do Christians so often shoot their wounded? Dwight is a Christian psychiatrist and his book gets straight to the problem of the wrong and *unhelpful* things some Christians think:

- No Christian who is right with God can have any kind of mental health issues.

- Anything that is wrong in someone's life is because they haven't confessed their sin to God.

- Even well-documented illnesses such as depression are seen as spiritual problems – we need to pray more, not go to our GP.

This is dangerous stuff, loading up vulnerable people with even more of a burden.

Giving the wrong impression

What can happen when Christians think like this is that it gives the wrong impression to hurting people about what faith and what being a Christian is. Some people in the stories in Section B rejected Christianity because of this – although for some it was only the rejection of being part of a church community; their faith remained strong. Some people who have been hurt turn to the church hoping to get help, but that doesn't always work out, because there are some aspects of church services that are difficult for people following trauma. These are some of the things people told me:

- "I just feel worse if I go to church – why would I want to do that?"

- "All that stuff about blood and putting the body of Jesus in my mouth is so utterly awful."

- "I don't feel safe in that church. I find that very upsetting, but if I do go, I just end up a shaking mass of jelly so I have to go home."

- "I sit in church and just feel so guilty and rejected. It's excruciating."

- "At that church they all want to touch me. I hate being touched."

- "It's too loud for me at church. I feel nervous and trembly if I go so I keep away. But I'm a Christian. I just don't want all those crowds now my memories have come back. I miss going but I just can't stand it. I wish they did a quiet service where I could just sit with my back to a wall with my teddy and hear soft music and let the love of Jesus flow into me. But it's not like that there. It's not like that anywhere I can find, but you'd have thought someone would work out that some people just need a quiet space, wouldn't you?"

Dividing people into two groups

Several books about forgiving declare that there are two groups of people:

- those who forgive, and
- those who hang onto old hates and become bitter and twisted – and by doing this they damage their spiritual life.

But I think there's a third group of people struggling, and probably a fourth group of others groping their way towards managing overwhelming emotions as their life changes for ever.

It's quite likely that there's a fifth group – even 100 groups, maybe – of people who are trying in their own unique ways to recover physically, emotionally, and spiritually.

Dividing people into just two groups is far too simplistic, and ignorant, denying the struggle and alienation that can come with facing a traumatic incident. As Robert Welch puts it in his book *Kicking the Black Mamba* about the death of his beloved son, "there isn't much space in the world for those who don't fit in".

If we divide people into the two groups above, we are leaving out vulnerable people who struggle to forgive – who find life in general difficult. Could we make more space in our churches for these people who don't fit in?

The wrong impression of Christianity

Through ignorance of the "disintegration of self" caused by trauma, some people give completely the wrong impression of the love and care that can be available for people in a church community. I was watching a television discussion last week in which a Hindu woman was insisting that in society now there is nowhere for people who are hurting. The Church of England bishop sitting next to her was saying that the church is still there for people.

He's right. But not always, and Philip Yancey explores this point at the start of his wonderful book *What's So Amazing About Grace?* He quotes a friend of his telling a story of a homeless, sick and hungry prostitute who was trying to get help to turn her life around. She had such an expensive drug habit that she was renting out her two-year-old daughter because that earned more in an hour than she could earn in a whole night with her clients.

Philip Yancey's friend goes on to say:

> At last I asked if she had ever thought of going to a church for help. I will never forget the look of pure naïve shock that crossed her face. "Church!" she cried. "Why would I ever go there? I was already feeling terrible about myself. They'd just make me feel worse."

Exactly! Why would she want to turn to the church?

Sometimes Christians are giving out the wrong messages, giving completely the wrong impression of Christianity. People flee from it – understandably. For Richard and Marion in chapter 3 the attitude from their church was all too much and they sought friendship and love elsewhere. I've talked to lots of people who simply don't want to be part of church communities because there's nothing there to "attract" them. No love for them that might draw them in.

This is a tragedy.

Repackage the good news

So what I'm suggesting, if you are in a position of supporting people who have been through some kind of traumatic experience, is that you repackage what you say to them. For example, focusing more on God's love is going to be both closer to the main message of the Bible, and also more likely to draw people into God's kingdom.

Forgiving can be healing – but only if it's seen as something that is:

- part of love
- talked about with a smile
- supported with the kind of compassion that Jesus had for hurt and rejected people.

Misconceptions

I found some people had quite profound misconceptions about what forgiving actually is. Often that is something negative.

- "I can't live with myself if I forgive him."
- "It feels as if I need to give up my last bit of self-respect if I forgive her."
- "But I don't want to have to say that what they did was OK. If I forgive them, I'm saying it wasn't wrong."
- "If I forgive him a part of me would die inside."
- "To forgive is to condone. So I will never forgive."

There are clear misconceptions here about what forgiving means. The "If you don't forgive, God won't forgive you!" threat plus misconceptions can only result in people fleeing from those who say that (understandably) but then maybe never hear of God's love for them. How will they find someone to help them put their burdens down?

It's crucial that these misconceptions are addressed when we are trying to help people struggling with letting go.

How can I help?

Most people are likely to need help to heave the biggest burdens out of their backpack. I asked some survivors of abuse what helps them when they are at church. They said it helps if people will:

- listen, without judging us
- not mind if we go over the traumatic event again and again
- not keep telling us we must forgive or God won't forgive us
- remind us that it is God who forgives and gives us the power to dump the bad stuff
- remind us that we are already forgiven and loved by God – and God can carry our burdens for us.

I would add to that list that people being positive is a huge help – welcoming, friendly – and maybe accepting that not all survivors can cope with church. There is some evidence that for every survivor of abuse who goes reasonably regularly to church, there are thirty who can't cope for a range of reasons.

Another issue I would add to the list is the importance of seeing forgiving from the point of view of the victim, not only from some theological standpoint we might hold. It's one of those times when we need to feel the weight of the backpack of the person we are trying to help. Also, when there have been threats around the word "forgive", it can help just to use the words "letting go", until the person is further along their healing journey.

I know from experience that helping survivors of abuse can be complex – and long-term – so it's possible that others who have faced trauma in a different way might respond similarly – needing long-term support.

Emotional baggage

If you've never been through a traumatic experience, you may not know the extent of the emotional damage some people live with. If you think back to some moment when you realized something has gone horribly wrong – perhaps a car accident which will mean that you can't get to school in time to pick up a child, and no way of contacting anyone to let them know – a sense of panic and helplessness can take over. Our tummy churns. Future plans have to be abandoned; the important appointment later in the day can't happen.

For people with "secure attachment" and a reasonably ordered life, the sense of panic may last only a few moments, but if you can think back to those awful moments in your life, I'm writing this to explain that many people traumatized in some way have that same sense of panic and powerlessness *all the time*.

So many times Christians have told me that I "should feel at peace" and there is "no need to fear". But for decades I felt extreme anxiety, fear and powerlessness all the time! It never went away. I'm a great deal better now, but it's important to recognize that many people struggling with forgiving live with some kind of emotional baggage that significantly affects the quality of their life. And it really isn't helpful just to say they should pray more for healing!

They are where they are at the moment in their journey.

Oh, you wouldn't say that

Last week a friend was asking me how I was getting on with this book and I said I was just doing the bit where I want to encourage clergy and others not to say, "If you don't forgive, God won't forgive you."

> Friend: Oh, but we must say that because God can't forgive us if we don't forgive.
>
> Me: But that's not a helpful thing to say to survivors of abuse.
>
> Friend: Oh, you wouldn't say that to a survivor! Of course not. It would be like abusing them all over again.

My friend who said this is a survivor of the most terrible abuse from her family and has herself been subjected to spiritual abuse including being told she "must forgive or else ..." So I really wasn't sure what to make of our conversation. But it is typical of thinking about forgiveness – woolly and not clearly thought through.

Who can we say it to?

So if it is seen as insensitive to say "If you don't forgive…" to survivors of abuse (a widely held view amongst people I talked to, including people who hadn't experienced trauma), then who could we say it to?

Would it be appropriate to say it to someone who is struggling to forgive when their life has been dramatically changed when:

- their child was murdered
- they were thrown into prison for standing up for justice and freedom
- they were tortured
- their house was burgled and deeply personal treasures were stolen?

Of course it would be inappropriate to say, "If you don't forgive, God won't forgive you!" to any of these people. Just as we wouldn't say to someone recently bereaved, "Buck up, every cloud has a silver lining."

But some Christians are saying that kind of thing to vulnerable people!

Remember, it isn't possible for people to rank difficult events that have happened to someone else because it isn't what actually happened that matters, it's the sense that the victim made of the event at the time. None of us can judge someone's reaction to an event. What appears minor to one person can be traumatic for another. So if you think someone is overreacting to what you think was a minor incident, remember that it could be world-shattering for them.

How are we heard?

So, when some kind of difficult incident happens, is it ever appropriate to threaten with "If you don't forgive, God…"? I don't think it is. It feels too judgmental – believing we can assess someone's standing with God. I also think it's verbal and sometimes spiritual bullying.

Also, my experience of talking to clergy and others about forgiving showed that some people think they don't say threatening things, but they actually do! Some people seem to think they talk about forgiving quite gently. But that's not the way they are heard.

We need to be aware that people who are vulnerable, whose thinking processes have been muddled by trauma, will almost always tend to think negatively, and sometimes will "hear" what you say through their "sieve" that can take out all the positive thoughts you think you are saying.

Vulnerable people can sometimes have low self-esteem, and an assumption that they are wrong about everything. (It took me decades to grow out of this.) So we need to take great care to be "over the top" careful about how we word any discussions, or sermons, about forgiving, or we risk being horribly misunderstood.

Talking to adults

I've had conversations with clergy where they insist they must say "you must forgive". I disagree. I think it is better to stop trying to fix things. Instead, *listen to people and come alongside them.*

- Where are they coming from?

- What are they struggling with?
- *What are they really saying* – that might not be what they are actually saying; there can often be something they are not able to say.

My friend Carolyn expressed this when I was working with her and a group of clergy recently:

> Sit back on the sofa and listen. Listen! Think about what the best response will be so that the person will not clam up, but will feel able to say what is really on their mind. Listen!

Judge not

The Bible is very clear that it isn't appropriate to judge another human being.

When I've said this to clergy, they sometimes say something along these lines:

"But I'm in the business of looking after souls. It's my job to tell people they must forgive."

But if we are caring for someone's soul, do we have to do it by threatening them? Wouldn't it be better to talk about God's love?

This is what I mean about repackaging what we say to people so we don't reject them and repel them.

> When we honestly ask ourselves which person in our lives means the most to us, we often find that it is those who, instead of giving much advice, solutions, or cures, have chosen rather to share our pain and touch our wounds with a gentle and tender hand. The friend who can be silent with us in a moment of despair or confusion, who can stay with

us in an hour of grief and bereavement, who can tolerate not knowing, not curing, not healing and face with us the reality of our powerlessness, that is a friend who cares.

(Henri Nouwen)

God loves you

Another situation I've found myself in is when someone is haranguing somebody with "You must forgive..." For example, a few years ago I went to talk to a newly formed group of depressed people. I set the group off with some workshop activities but the woman next to me, Myra, burst into tears and said she was depressed because her sister had died of cancer and while dying had desperately wanted to see her mother. But her father refused to allow the mother to go to her. There had been a long history of sexual abuse in the family and when the sister, as a young person, had disclosed that her father had sexually abused her, he threw the sister out of the house and said that no one in the family was to have contact with her.

Because the father always denied doing anything wrong there was never an apology and the sister found it hard to forgive her father. (Understandably.)

Myra knew that her sister's accusations of abuse were right because the father started abusing Myra when the sister left. He told Myra that if she said anything about the abuse, she too would be sent away and would never see her mother again.

Now Myra was in tears because she had been to a Lent course at her church, and had been told, "If you don't forgive, God won't forgive you!"

"But I can't forgive my father for not letting my sister hold her mother's hand as she died."

I sat next to Myra and tried to talk her through the huge misconception that she had that God would reject her. But another person, Fiona, launched into telling Myra that she must forgive or God couldn't possibly forgive her.

Through her tears Myra asked the obvious question about whether her sister – who had not been able to forgive the father – had gone to hell. "Well ..." said Fiona, clearly meaning "yes". This was far too much for me! I launched into battle with Fiona, who was citing Matthew 18 and the Lord's Prayer as evidence that God would not forgive Myra's sister.

Myra continued to weep uncontrollably.

I knew that comforting Myra was my top priority and as I argued what the Lord's Prayer actually meant Myra continued to cry.

"God loves you, Myra. He's not going to reject you – or your sister," I said.

Fiona eventually agreed that Myra needed to remember that God loved her. The astonishing thing is that Fiona is usually a lovely, caring person – just not around issues of forgiveness! I don't think she realized how incredibly hurtful her words were that day.

Responding with compassion

I've told this story here to demonstrate what I mean about our need to repackage what we say to people. I was angry with Fiona for putting Myra through all those tears. It seems to me that people who are upset about an incident need to hear about God's love, not threats.

Of course, we all want to be able to say what we think – what we believe that the Bible is saying, just as I am in this book, but I think we must be careful about judging. I think it is inappropriate to tell someone they are heading for hell. It's judging people in a way I don't think any human being – clergy or otherwise – has the right to do. It's God who decides about people's souls. Not us.

But I'm aware as I say that, I was in danger of judging Fiona when I was so angry with her. And I'm aware that some people reading this will think that she was right to suggest that Myra was heading for hell.

But I beg you, even if you really believe that people such as Myra – those who struggle to forgive – actually are heading for hell, to try to re-word things and focus more on God's love for all of us, rather than the threat.

The threats are so damaging. From my research for this book, it seems it is the threats that put hurting people off Christianity. Threats add to people's burdens.

Joy and contentment?

Some of the books I read about forgiving had a rather worrying tendency to say that if we could only forgive, joy, peace, and contentment would be ours and we would ride off into the sunset and live happily ever after. This is incredibly unreal if it's seen as a blueprint for everyone.

But is anyone's life really like that? I feel hugely contented with my life and, of course, at times I feel full of joy and so excited to be alive. But much of life is a struggle. I'm sure it's true that "forgiving is good for you", but it does only reflect a part of our complex lives.

I think we do a disservice to people to intimate that they "should" be joyful and contented – and if we're not it just shows that we need to forgive more! This is seriously faulty thinking, and it's guilt-inducing and unreal for those in recovery from a traumatic hurt.

Feeling free

If I look back at my own forgiving journey, I can see that joy and contentment have grown as I've matured and come to terms with some of my difficult issues. But the dominant feeling I have is a sense of gradually becoming free from some of the post-traumatic stress symptoms. So I want to suggest that it might be better to support people who are struggling more with an aim that they might gradually *feel free* – less burdened – rather than suggesting they should feel joyful. This sense of being freed is a point that Stephen Cherry makes in his wonderful book *Healing Agony*:

> If only the free and creative can forgive, and we think
> that forgiveness is a good thing, then our project is not to
> press people to forgive but to empower them to be free.
> And one way in which people can free themselves and
> others is through forgiveness. If this sounds circular, it is.
> Forgiveness and freedom together create a virtuous circle,
> or spiral.
>
> (Stephen Cherry)

Forgiving can be hard

Forgiving is healing – but it can be difficult; it can feel impossible for some – and we need to accept that that is where that person is at that moment. Haranguing them simply isn't helpful.

Some people need lots of help to find ways to put down these huge burdens, and it is us sharing the compassion of Jesus that is that help. If there is only one thing you remember from the whole of this book, I hope it will be this:

Instead of saying "You must forgive, or God won't forgive you!", it would be much more healing for people to say:

"Forgiving can be hard, but I will walk with you as you try to let go. I'll be there to help you. Remember that God loves you. That's where we all start our journey. God loves you and nothing can ever separate you from that love."

Resources

Forgiveness

David W. Augsburger, *Helping People Forgive*, Louisville, KY: Westminster John Knox Press, 1996

Anthony Bash, *Just Forgiveness: Exploring the Bible, Weighing the Issues*, London: SPCK, 2011

Stephen Cherry, *Healing Agony: Re-imagining Forgiveness*, London: Continuum, 2012

Dennis Linn, Sheila Fabricant Linn, Matthew Linn, *Don't Forgive Too Soon*, New York: Paulist Press, 1997

Alistair McFadyen and Marcel Sarot, eds, *Forgiveness and Truth*, Edinburgh: T & T Clark, 2001

Jim McManus and Stephanie Thornton, *Finding Forgiveness*, Chawton: Redemptorist Press, 2006

John Monbourquette, *How to Forgive: A Step-by-step Guide*, London: Darton Longman & Todd, 2000 (English translation)

Jeffrie G. Murphy, *Getting Even: Forgiveness and its Limits*, New York: OUP, 2004

F. LeRon Shults and Stephen J. Sandage, *The Faces of Forgiveness*, Grand Rapids: Baker Academic, 2003

Lewis Smedes, *The Art of Forgiving*, Nashville, TN: Moorings, 1996

Lewis Smedes, *Forgive and Forget*, San Francisco: Harper & Row, 1984

Miroslav Volf, *Free of Charge*, Grand Rapids: Zondervan, 2005

Miroslav Volf, *Exclusion and Embrace*, Nashville: Abingdon Press, 1996

Fraser Watts and Liz Gulliford, eds, *Forgiveness in Context: Theology and Psychology in Creative Dialogue*, London: T & T Clark, 2004

Gordon Wilson and Alf McCreary, *Marie: A Story from Enniskillen*, London: Marshall Pickering, 1990

The Forgiveness Project, http://theforgivenessproject.com/ (accessed 12 March 2014)

Cognitive behavioural therapy

Stephen Briars, *Brilliant Cognitive Behavioural Therapy*, London: Pearson, 2009 (this is a really helpful and easy to use book)

There are websites such as MoodGYM, and Living Life to the Full, and these are both worth looking at. MoodGYM (https://moodgym.anu.edu.au/welcome) is specifically for those who are depressed, and Living Life to the Full www.llttf.com/index.php?section=page&page_seq=8 is more general. Both are free.

Limbic lag

Michael Dye wrote "Relapse and the Brain" on the The Genesis Process website. This website is very helpful for understanding a range of things, particularly limbic lag and how to work at lessening the impact of it. www.genesisprocess.org/understanding-relapse

Recovery from abuse

S:vox, a UK group of survivors on Facebook. For contact:
http://reshapers.org.uk/transformation/

Healing Weeks for Survivors of Abuse: Heal for Life Foundation,
www.healforlife.org.uk and in Australia, www.healforlife.com.au

Sue Atkinson, *Breaking the Chains of Abuse*, Oxford: Lion Hudson,
2006

Understanding grooming

Jane Grayshon, *Goodbye Pink Room*, Oxford: Lion Hudson, 2014

This is a difficult read for survivors of abuse but it shows clearly how
grooming, as a prelude to childhood sexual abuse, can take place. It
also shows how well intentioned Christian parents can actually make
the situation worse for the child.

Books on other topics

Carol J. Adams and Marie M. Fortune, eds, *Violence against Women
and Children: A Christian Theological Sourcebook*, New York:
Continuum, 1995

Dietrich Bonhoeffer, *The Cost of Discipleship*, London: SCM, 1959

Joan Borysenko, *Fire in the Soul*, New York: Grand Central
Publishing, 1994

Brother John of Taizé, *Praying the Our Father*, Portland, Oregon: The
Pastoral Press, 1992

Lucia Capacchione, *Recovery of Your Inner Child*, New York: Simon & Schuster 1991

Dwight L. Carlson, *Why Do Christians Shoot Their Wounded?*, Carlisle: OM Publishing, 1994

Barbara Glasson, *A Spirituality of Survival: Enabling a Response to Trauma and Abuse*, London: Continuum, 2009

Judith Herman, *Trauma and Recovery: The Aftermath of Violence – from Domestic Abuse to Political Terror*, New York: Basic Books, 1997

Kate Litchfield, *Tend my Flock*, Norwich: Canterbury Press, 2006

Peter Longson, *God in the Dark*, Glasgow: Wild Goose Publications, 2012

Nancy J. Napier, *Getting Through the Day*, New York: W. W. Norton & Company, 1994

Julie Nicholson, *A Song for Jenny*, London: HarperCollins, 2010

Henri Nouwen, *Out of Solitude*, Notre Dame, IN: Ave Maria Press, 1973

Eugene H. Peterson, *The Message: The New Testament in Contemporary Language*, Colorado Springs: NavPress Publishing Group, 1993

John Powell, *Why Am I Afraid to Tell You Who I Am?* Grand Rapids: Zondervan, 1999

Paula Radcliffe, *How to Run*, London: Simon & Schuster, 1997

Susan Shooter, *How Survivors of Abuse Relate to God*, Farnham: Ashgate, 2012

Lewis Smedes, *Shame and Grace*, London: SPCK, 1993

Fraser Watts, Rebecca Nye and Sara Savage, *Psychology for Christian*

Ministry, London: Routledge, 2002

Robert Welch, *Kicking the Black Mamba: Life, Alcohol and Death*, London: DLT, 2012

Walter Wink, *Engaging the Powers: Discernment and Resistance in a World of Domination*, Minneapolis: Fortress Press 1992

Tom Wright, *The Lord and His Prayer*, London: SPCK, 1996

Tom Wright, *Surprised by Hope*, London: SPCK, 2007

Tom Wright, *Matthew for Everyone, parts 1 and 2*, London: SPCK, 2002

Philip Yancey, *What's So Amazing About Grace?*, Grand Rapids: Zondervan, 1997

Philip Yancey, *Where is God When it Hurts?*, London: Marshall Pickering, 1977.

Churches Together in Britain and Ireland, *Time for Action: Sexual Abuse, the Churches and a New Dawn for Survivors*, London: CTBI, 2002; available from the CTBI website www.ctbi.org.uk/253/

Common Worship, London: Church House Publishing, 2005

Church of England reports

Responding Well, Church House Publishing, 2011 www.churchofengland.org/media/1292643/respondingwellforweb. pdf (accessed 12 March 2014)

Protecting All God's Children (safeguarding policy for children and young people, 4th edition, November 2010) www.churchofengland. org/media/37378/protectingallgodschildren.pdf (accessed 12 March 2014)

Promoting a Safe Church (safeguarding policy for adults, 2006, updated in 2012) www.churchofengland.org/media/37405/promotingasafechurch.pdf (accessed 12 March 2014)

Responding to Domestic Abuse (guidelines for those with pastoral responsibility, 2006) www.churchofengland.org/media/1163604/domesticabuse.pdf (accessed 12 March 2014)

Bishop Paul Butler, General Synod Report of Proceedings July 2013 www.churchofengland.org/ (accessed 19 March 2014)

Other websites

Gordon Wilson quote: www.bbc.co.uk/news/20257328 (accessed 19 March 2014)

Martin Niemöller quote: www.history.ucsb.edu/faculty/marcuse/niem.htm (accessed 19 March 2014)

Michael Dye, "Relapse and the Brain": www.genesisprocess.org/understanding-relapse (accessed 19 March 2014)

www.churchofengland.org/clergy-office-holders/child-protection-safeguarding/speech-from-bishop-paul-butler-at-july-2013-synod.aspx (accessed 12 March 2014)

Note:
Singapore Story is a 1950s film about the war story of Bishop Leonard Wilson. His daughter, Revd Canon Susan Cole-King referred to it in her homily at the Lambeth Conference, 7 August 1998.